Cesar Pelli

Cesar Pelli

BY JOHN PASTIER

MONOGRAPHS IN CONTEMPORARY ARCHITECTURE

WHITNEY LIBRARY OF DESIGN, an imprint of Watson-Guptill Publications/New York

GRANADA London Toronto Sydney New York

First published 1980 in New York by Whitney Library of Design,
an imprint of Watson-Guptill Publications,
a division of Billboard Publications, Inc.,
1515 Broadway, New York, N.Y. 10036

Library of Congress Cataloging in Publication Data
Pastier, John, 1939-
   Cesar Pelli.
   (Monographs on contemporary architecture)
   1. Pelli, Cesar.   2. Architecture, Modern — 20th
century — United States.   I. Series.
NA737.P39P37   720'.92'4   80-17317
ISBN 0-8230-7414-5

First published in Great Britain 1981 by Granada Publishing
Granada Publishing — Technical Books Division
Frogmore, St Albans, Herts AL2 2NF
and
3 Upper James Street, London W1R 4BP
117 York Street, Sydney, NSW 2000, Australia
PO Box 84165, Greenside, 2034 Johannesburg, South Africa
61 Beach Road, Auckland, New Zealand
ISBN 0-246-11504-1
Granada®
Granada Publishing®

Manufactured in U.S.A.

First Printing, 1980

Edited by Sharon Lee Ryder and Susan Davis
Designed by Vienne + Lehmann-Haupt

Contents

ACKNOWLEDGMENTS

Several people deserve thanks for their help in bringing this book into being. Foremost is Cesar Pelli, who repeatedly found time within a demanding schedule to discuss far more buildings, ideas, and details than have managed to make their way onto these pages and who has been supportive of an independent viewpoint in circumstances where many other architects would have encouraged a mere restatement of their own thoughts and beliefs.

Sandra Delaney, Fred Clarke, and Ken Champlin of Cesar Pelli & Associates and Stuart Lottman of Gruen Associates have been patient and indispensible in providing information and graphic material, and Randy Mudge, Tom Morton, and Jon Pickard of the Pelli office have explained projects still in evolution. At the Whitney Library, Lee Ryder envisioned both the book and the series of which it is a part, and she and Susan Davis have nurtured, questioned, and clarified the manuscript under hectic circumstances of my own making. Tyler Owlglass has been a voluble, if somewhat erratic, sounding board and grammarian.

Introduction

Architecture as a Reasonable Art

Hearing Cesar Pelli describe himself as "very much a pragmatist" conjures up visions of Arturo Toscanini calling himself a bandleader. After all, pragmatic architects are known to cut their fees, work too quickly, be ruled by their clients, and produce what are considered terrible buildings by many of their peers as well as the critics.

But Pelli's self-description, while deceptively incomplete, is basically accurate. He is no prima donna who needs lavish fees and leisurely schedules to turn out his work. He has spent most of his career directing design for large commercial firms, operating on lean rations of time and budget, and serving clients seeking economical, utilitarian buildings rather than architectural monuments. Playing by those tight rules, he has been able to deliver structures that usually surmount their limitations and often attain the level of high-art architecture.

Such a performance requires a special genius, and much of it can be attributed to an extraordinary clearheadedness about the potentialities of each project. When given a sow's ear, Pelli will try to stretch the capability of pigskin rather than take refuge in dreams of silk. He is untempted by chimeral design possibilities, seemingly immune to games of ego, well organized in his design system, and intellectually efficient. In these respects, Cesar Pelli is rational man personified.

Like his pragmatism, however, his logic and discipline do not tell the full story. He is also a visual hedonist, lavish in the use of color, quirky shapes, sleek surfaces, and at times even illusion. Pelli's architectural oeuvre can be viewed as a succession of encounters between the realist and the romantic, or the logician and the poet. Some have been dominated by one of these alter egos (more often the rationalist), some have been polite accommodations between the two, and still others have been inspired dialogues.

This duality, of course, has always been inherent in architecture, and at its best, design has always been a symbiosis of reason and intuition, of technical considerations and expressive ones. In our increasingly specialized and fragmented age, however, architects have been gravitating to one or another of those poles, and synthesis is not the norm. Eero Saarinen, for whom Pelli worked from 1954 to1964, was one of the exceptions. His most memorable method of linking those opposites was to enlist a heroic technology to achieve a poetic vision, a tactic clearly demonstrated in the TWA Terminal at New York's Kennedy Airport. Pelli was closely involved with this building, just as he was with the Stiles and Morse Colleges at Yale where technological innovation was put to less obvious use. There, unlike TWA, the building form was guided strongly by its context, and the special construction techniques involved producing a concrete masonry surface compatible with Yale's meticulous but no longer affordable Gothic revival stonework. In both of these cases, whatever their differences, the techniques used were indispensable

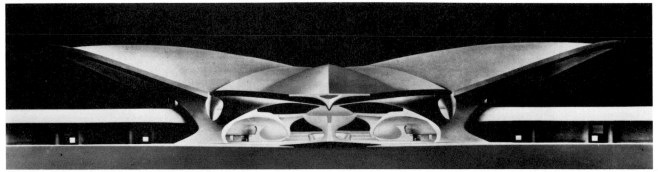

Eero Saarinen's TWA Terminal in New York uses massive amounts of concrete to express the idea of flight.

devices to effect desired formal results, just as mirror glass was developed specifically for Saarinen so that his Bell Telephone Laboratories could be all glass yet not a hothouse.

Pelli's approach is less pioneering. He will adjust the components of an evolving design to meet the properties of known technologies, thereby producing a seemingly effortless accommodation. This practice is not merely his way of using materials and building techniques, but part of a larger strategy encompassing the entire process of design. That outlook is best stated in Pelli's own words:

"I have always felt, unquestionably, that there is strength and energy flowing all around us. There is energy in the projects themselves, and I like to tap that energy and not fight it.

"It is not mystical. There are certain directions that the project wants to go. If you follow them, the project can go very far because it will be sustained by financial reasons, by construction needs, and by emotional preferences, and therefore gain the support of many critical and important people representing those different aspects of the problem.

"It is also true that there is great energy in the ideas that are common to your own time. Those are the ideas that are being discussed, are being elaborated, and are being explored. There are certain things that each period

searches out, and those are the areas where you can do most. There, in those channels, is where the water flows.

"I energize myself immensely by using this internal strength. It makes me feel I can do a lot more. It is not a metaphor—this strength is very real. It is the support of real people who make real decisions. Agreement is energy: it allows you to go much further. If you go in the direction where people will support you, you will not only use all of your own energies, but you will also use theirs. If you go in the direction where they will oppose you, you will have to spend energies just to overcome their objections and you're still not going to get all you wanted.

"That's energy. I feel that it allows your work to be more important and better, given your resources and capacity."

Pelli stresses that this set of perceptions is one that works well for him, but is not a universal prescription. He recognizes and respects those colleagues whose strong internal belief in their own ideas forms the basis of their architecture. Of course he too has ideas that consistently mold his designs, for even though there are "directions that the project wants to go," it won't go there without him, just as Louis Kahn's insights into "what the building wants to be" were finally ascribable to the designer and not the building. Pelli calls those ideas "tilts" and defines them as the particular inclinations that enter into the design process once the "demands, dimensions, and possibilities of the

problem are thoroughly understood."

When asked to identify his tilts, Pelli responds that "they are not concrete and . . . the strongest ones are invisible." Pressed further, he says that he wants his buildings to be "responsive to users, open to change and participation, and be good workable products." These, of course, are goals that many, if not most, contemporary architects would endorse in their own work, and they are not the particular ones that make Pelli's buildings most identifiable as his own. Granted, it is not easy for any individual to identify his own essential traits, but in this case there may also be a conjurer's reluctance to reveal his methods in detail.

Many of the tilts are obvious: Pelli loves internal order and clarity, the external ambiguities and distortions inherent in glass skins, as well as calculated irregularity inside and out. He enjoys using color and is sensitive to the dynamic aspects of a building, whether they be the motion of people through its spaces or a strategy for accommodating future growth. It also seems true that entirely new tilts are emerging at this point in his career, and will only become evident through later buildings and the passage of time.

However, there are two tilts of a different order that seem to be the motive forces behind his design inclinations, just as those inclinations are shapers of his buildings. These overriding inclinations—or perhaps they are one, as yang and yin are one—warrant attention before any of their more concrete offspring.

BASIC INCLINATIONS:
THE INTERPLAY OF ART AND SCIENCE

Cesar Pelli's fundamental inclination is not a simple plane, but a complex surface of opposed curvatures: one is abstract, rational, hard, and virtually scientific; the other is referential, romantic, intuitive, and poetic. This duality is not one of perfectly balanced opposites, and although the proportion varies among buildings and seems

Toronto-Dominion Tower in Vancouver seems to dissolve in a bank of clouds.

Sensuous column covers are the distinguishing feature of the General Telephone Building in Santa Monica.

to be shifting with time, the intellectual, left-brain forces have so far had a stronger mark on his work than the emotional, right-brain ones.

That one of the pair is dominant, and that it is the will to order, should not be surprising, since 20th-century architecture has been inclined to the stoic and has not encouraged a full synthesis of intellect and feeling. That stoicism has provoked a postmodernist backlash which is just as shortsighted in its rejection of reason as orthodox modernism was in its denial of sentiment. To the degree that his head rules his heart, Pelli is the 20th-century architect incarnate, but the recurring and apparently increasing presence of sensuous elements in his work also marks a fruitful middle ground between the older orthodoxy and the current fashion for caricature historicism.

The rigor and precision of his designs not only derive from the modern architectural tradition, but also reflect an avid interest in science and a strong respect for its methods. A substantial portion of his current information is scientific: besides professional journals, the five magazines on his regular reading list are *The New Scientist, Scientific American, The Economist, Newsweek*, and *The New York Review of Books*. More than once, in long clamorous discussions about the merits and limitations of science, he has held his own against a generally united front of his wife Diana, sons Denis (a physicist) and Rafael, and myself, while propounding that the scientific method is the most humble and effective road to truth yet devised. He admires this process for its self-correcting nature, objectivity and freedom from dogma, nonproprietary character, and innate ability to build up and refine a body of knowledge.

Many of those scientific values seem implicit in his own view of architecture as a cumulative societal process: he sees some of his design explorations as "experiments that can contribute to a general learning within the profession," just as he in turn has learned from the work of others, and he feels that "all architects have a general duty to contribute to the betterment of architecture." In addition to being a

Century City Medical Center curtain wall reflects nearby apartment building.

model for such professional interchange, science provides enjoyment, discovery, and intellectual stimulation. "It's more fun for me [than reading about art] . . . I find it an adventure. I have not one hair of a scientist—I am purely a dilettante."

The objective, rational aspects of Pelli's work stand out clearest in buildings produced in the dozen years after leaving Saarinen's office when he was head of design for two large, established Los Angeles firms: first Daniel, Mann, Johnson and Mendenhall (DMJM) from 1964 to 1968 and then Gruen Associates (originally Victor Gruen Associates) from 1968 to 1976. It was in Los Angeles that

Pelli demonstrated a fascination for abstract, crystalline glass skins, and it was there that he formulated and refined a flexible organizational system based on circulation spines. In perhaps a dozen of his earliest buildings these two recurring themes, singly or in combination, provided most of the design interest within a given project. As new ideas they perforce began simply, but that simplicity was also enforced by brisk design schedules and generally stringent construction budgets. Rationalism and simplicity were also fostered by a need to justify design directions to entrepreneurial clients and even in some degree to the management of his own organizations, since prior to Pelli's working for the two corporations, their

accomplishments in that area had been dependably mundane.

Nevertheless, there was still opportunity for Pelli's other side to surface as well. Even in his first year in California, he employed strong colors and devised forms and spaces of baroque complexity. The taut and formally precise glass skins also had their sensuous aspects, in that their mirrored or darkly reflective surfaces threw back changing images of their surroundings, often warped or fragmented into new patterns. In the early Gruen years there were experiments where strong colors virtually carried the design of a fast-food outlet and a department store restaurant. Later works used colors in either subtler or more confidently reductivist fashion, while quirky hybrid shapes added richness to what had earlier been elemental building profiles and interior spaces.

But it is only in his most recent independent projects that Pelli's intuitive side has emerged strongly and consistently enough to balance the omnipresent rationalist foundation of his work. With the house for the 1976 Venice Biennale, which is as much a work of conceptual art as it is of architecture, there begins a foray into new imagery, playful homage to other architecture (previously, any architectural allusions were straightfaced adaptations, mainly of his own works), and an evident sense of new freedom and self-confidence. These qualities are currently manifest in a varied collection of apartment and office towers designed since 1979.

It seems, therefore, that Pelli's fundamental and dualistic tilt is itself tilting. The steeply curved slopes between science and art, analysis and lyrical expression, are leveling out and the peaks are becoming more equal in magnitude. There is still a stimulating contrast between the two, but it is now joined by a greater sense of affinity.

INCLINATIONS TOWARD CHANGE

The logic and clarity of science are reflected in Pelli's treatment of buildings as mutable entities. Circulation spines were one of his earliest predilections, providing a rationale to organize complicated building programs and also allow for later growth and transformation. Typically, spaces of one functional category were attached to one side of a central corridor and those of a different nature plugged in on the other. Expansion could occur along the spine or at right angles to it, either outward or upward.

The linear connector, generously sized and commanding outward views, became the main social and architectural space of a design, duplicating in form and purpose the classic urban street. Sometimes a secondary passage would be provided parallel to the first, and the two, along with their cross-passages, would form an analogue to a city street grid. Indeed, after using the spine in laboratory complexes for Teledyne and COMSAT, Pelli expanded the idea to serve as the basis for Open-Line City, a hypothetical urban-planning strategy anchored upon a public transportation line and capable of open-ended growth.

As an architectural system it reached its most dramatic form in the winning but unbuilt competition project for Vienna's

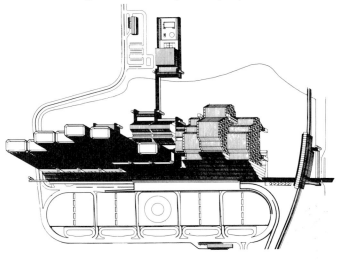

UN City brings the spine principle to its ultimate architectural form.

UN City, arguably Pelli's finest design, where it was developed at monumental scale and elaborated along several axes. Ingenious and intellectually solid, the spine principle reflects its Los Angeles nativity in that it works best on large sites and in clean-slate contexts, and these restrictions would be more pronounced and far more limiting if the concept were applied at a metropolitan scale.

Conversely, it has served very well, at least in theory, on the intimate scale of a single dwelling. In his last building designed in Los Angeles, a house project for the 1976 Venice Biennale done independently of the Gruen organization, Pelli used the spine to exploit the dimension of time no less than those of space. Free to devise any program, he envisioned a massive central gallery as the only fixed element of a lifelong construction sequence molded by changing patterns of use, fluctuating family size, and eventual urbanization of the originally pastoral setting. The result is as much a narrative as a building, a

Shaped tops of Four Leaf Towers in Houston give character to an otherwise straightforward design.

14

parable of life and society in which the architectural forms are diagrammatic and the guiding principle is transformation.

But open-ended spines are not the only expression of flux in Pelli's architecture: growth, change, and a fascination for things unfinished are implicit in yet others of his buildings. The Columbus, Indiana, Commons and Courthouse Center embraces a large public space that gains meaning largely through the people it attracts and the variety of activities it can accommodate. This inherently fluctuating character is encapsulated in its Jean Tinguely sculpture *Chaos*, which goes into sonic and kinetic paroxysms at regular intervals. Fox Hills Mall, a California shopping center, is of necessity a closed-ended spine, but it still achieves a dynamic sense by the offset linkage of two levels of stores on one side with three on the other. The Pacific Design Center is not meant to change, but seems predicated in some part on the assumption that its fine-grained surroundings would do so in the future. Presently successful as a free-standing architectural space, the Niagara Falls Winter Garden is planned to open out into future stores. But even then, its sliced-off ends and thrusting profile will make it appear capable of extension, and therefore not necessarily complete.

In one respect, however, Pelli has begun departing from one widespread modern practice of leaving buildings unfinished. Among his current highrise projects, several display shaped tops or even spires that give finality to forms usually halted in midflight.

TECHNOLOGICAL INCLINATIONS

Being conversant with science, Pelli understands what many other designers do not: high-tech architecture is pretty much a myth. Even before the term was so badly debased by its linkage with commercial-grade cookware and the sado-masochistic look in home furnishing, it was rarely used with any understanding of the forms and capabilities of present technology. True high-tech is

The spire atop a proposed Pittsburgh office building departs from normal functionalist practice.

exemplified by such efforts as the space program, and even the more advanced methods used in building construction are clearly crude in comparison. What exists, Pelli points out, is really "nothing more than an expression of high technology used for artistic purposes."

Defining building technology as "simply the way in which materials are used and labor is organized," he obviously sees it more as a means than as an expressive end. He uses industrialized materials and methods both because they reflect our society and because they are usually the most practical way to build in an age of tight schedules, high costs, and low skills.

At the same time, he clearly delights in some of the visual possibilities of architectural technology. His optimistic rationalism resembles that of the great Victorian engineers, and like them Pelli has an instinct for trusswork and a fondness for grand spaces flooded with light from transparent roofs and walls. He admires the Crystal Palace and calls it "the first major piece of architecture to be built around the limitations and possibilities of our epoch."

There is one particular aspect of building technology with which he has been identified so strongly that it is virtually synonymous with his name. And if this were the age of Caesar it would be literally so, for in Latin *pelli* is the dative singular of the word "skin." Whether this fact will add weight to the thesis that architecture obeys the laws of linguistics is not certain, but there is no doubt that the expressive possibilities of architectural skin have been amply demonstrated by this man who shares its name.

Starting with the Century City Medical Center, Pelli has tenaciously explored ways of expressing lightweight enclosures freed from structural tasks: His favorite material in this quest has been glass: "Because you need to build windows, the glass part of the building is almost given." Granted, the wall sections not needed for light or view could be made of metal, plastic, or even properly detailed concrete and still visually express their nonstructural nature.

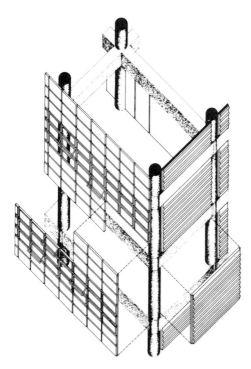

Scored concrete panels enclose the U.S. Embassy at Tokyo in the visual spirit of light Japanese screens.

Pelli has used steel, aluminum, and grooved concrete in those roles, but finds glass is "more economical, adaptable, readily available, and has wonderful properties." Esthetically, those qualities include transparency, opacity, and reflectivity, and over the years his applications of the material have exploited them to their fullest. For example, he has used the smallest possible exterior mullions or gaskets to hold the panes together and has often beveled the corners to strengthen the idea of a continuous taut membrane covering the building. Pelli would quite likely clad his structures in a single, huge glass sheet, or perhaps even shrink-wrap them, if such things were technologically feasible.

He pursues skins out of a perceived need for a contemporary esthetic system to replace the one that grew out of masonry construction and that still has a hold on our perceptions. He seeks to supplant the older visual values of mass, depth, and implied permanence with a "post-masonry architecture" of volume, surface, and transiency: "a flower, not a stone."

To that end, Pelli has relied most on the reflective qualities of the material, and in some cases he has produced dazzlingly complex sequences of multiple images. He finds mirrored glass insufficiently subtle and prefers dark tints that balance reflectivity with opacity and transparency at far lower cost. He has used glass in gray, brown, mirrored silver, and even a rich opaque blue; has explored various ways of holding it in place; and has wrapped it around square corners, chamfers, and faceted curves. There have been times that he felt close to exhausting the material's possibilities, but he does not feel so now. In two current designs, Four Leaf Towers and the Museum of Modern Art, he is using elaborate multicolored curtain wall patterns that hover somewhere between a tartan and a Mondrian.

Beyond esthetics, he is highly conscious of glass's reputation, not always deserved, as an energy-waster. This, of course, is a problem of economics: so far most architects have been financially constrained to design thermally porous wall systems. However, Pelli has an unusual opportunity in an office-building commission for the state of California in Sacramento. The State Architect's office has been a forceful advocate of energy-effective design, and Pelli's response to the problem may prove to be a surprising one.

But, energy aside, there are other questions about the material. Used as a building's sole external cladding, glass has its limits, and two bear mention here. For one, although the glass skins of Pelli and many other architects are often beautiful and inspire seductive photography, they do not always look that way. In the wrong weather or at the wrong times of day, they lack reflectivity and reveal an uninspiring collage of blinds, drapes, and light fixtures behind their windows. Perhaps this expresses time and

occupancy, but it is not a scene that any architect will allow in his brochure or slide shows. Furthermore, nonmirrored skins are reflective only at sharp angles, and the customary artful photos show images not visible from many vantage points. Glass skins have their sunset moments of sublimity, but are also prone to stretches of banality. Masonry architecture holds out fewer surprises, but also fewer inconsistencies of appearance.

The other limitation of glass is that it is not always an endearing substance. Its nature—hard, crisp, cool, and slick—is that of ice, and as one of the materials of choice, along with metal, for housing large, impersonal organizations, it has become a popular symbol of indifference and alienation. Admittedly, this connotation can be dispelled by proper design, but when a glass building falls short of excellence (and Pelli has not been completely immune to such lapses), that unsympathetic aspect of glass comes to the fore. Probably sensing these inherent drawbacks, he has become more inclined to combine glass with spandrels of other material and, when using it alone, has introduced pattern or abstract imagery on surfaces that once went unadorned.

INCLINATIONS IN THE REALM OF THE SENSES

Beyond being disciplined technological exercises, glass skins are capable of a strong sensory aspect.

Their fleeting reflections speak at least as much to the eyes as to the mind, and when used on a highly shaped building such as the Pacific Design Center, they seem to take on a tactile quality. That one design, in fact, embodies nearly all Pelli's inclinations that engage the senses. The building is wrapped in a rich blue skin, and its great bulk has, if anything, been rendered more corporeal by its odd form. Its local nickname, the "Blue Whale," aptly describes its huge and palpably animated presence. A slightly askew siting, used more strongly in the Tokyo Embassy, and a fearlessly asymmetrical profile common to many of Pelli's works give it an external dynamism beyond that of reflectivity and hue.

Inside it is equally alive. Pelli's opportunities to build memorable public spaces have not been frequent—the Columbus Commons, the Security Pacific Bank, the Winter Garden, and the Fox Hills Mall are the other happy exceptions—but the internal cavities of the Blue Whale would entice even Jonah and Pinocchio into a second visit. The corridors wander amiably, a wide lobby slides diagonally through the building's full width, and a huge barrel-glazed galleria runs the length of the upper two floors. A pair of escalator banks is treated three-dimensionally, and the main stack, set in a glass-fronted cylinder, provides a deft synthesis of panoramic city views, natural light, abstract geometry, and a pavane-like passage through time and space.

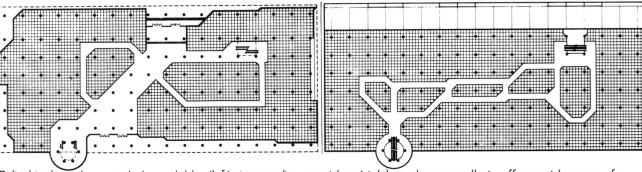

Cylindrical escalator stack, lower lobby (left), intermediate corridors (right), and upper galleria offer a wide range of spatial experiences to users of Pacific Design Center in Los Angeles.

Daehan Kyoyuk Insurance Company's barrel vault and window wall are descendants of Pacific Design Center galleria.

The Blue Whale summarizes Pelli's major sensory leanings, but some deserve further mention in terms of his other works. Color and light are foremost among these, and it is fair to say that Pelli is one of the prime colorists among contemporary architects. His palette ranges from the inspired blatancy of the Blue Whale to the soft tones of the Fox Hills Mall interior and the polychromatic intricacies of the Museum of Modern Art and Four Leaf Towers curtain walls.

Within the Security Pacific Bank in San Bernardino is the most intriguing example of color in any Pelli design, one that is the work of his wife, Diana Balmori, who is an architect and a professor of Latin American history. It is a four-story abstraction of the Santa Monica sky at sunset in the form of a graded wash that runs from blue through faint green, yellow, orange, and almost to red. Executed by film-industry scene painters, it is not a mural but actually the interior color scheme for the walls, columns, spandrel beams, and tellers' counters. On the outside, the idea is further abstracted: the first floor is clad in dull orange tile, and the three above in bluish-gray.

If the notion of sunset can be encoded in tile, so can that of geography. Pelli designed a prototypical exterior of stainless-steel trimmed ceramic tile for the Ohrbachs store chain, whereby each location would be differentiated through color alone. Two California branches have been built: blue in Del Amo and maroon in Cerritos. Unfortunately, there are no firm plans for stores in Redlands or Orange County.

Light, of course, is indispensable for the perception of color just as it is of space. Pelli has used glass not just to create sheer membranes of enclosure, but also to illuminate the major spaces and colors of his interiors. The techniques are basic: toplighting in the shopping centers (conventional at Columbus, inventive at Fox Hills), north-facing window walls in the Security Pacific Bank, and a combination of the two in the Pacific Design Center galleria.

But there is also a reverse phenomenon: instead of natural light from outside defining a space for an observer within, at night those same spaces are defined by artificial light from inside for an observer outdoors. This occurs dramatically at the Commons and the Winter Garden, and it can be argued that both buildings look best after dark when, like vast aquariums, their glass enclosures seem to embrace and give form to a warm liquid illumination aswim with plants and people.

A final inclination in the realm of the senses has to do with stance and posture: several of Pelli's buildings, and often the best ones, have a distinct body language. Within a self-defined world of pragmatism, he allows himself occasional forays into anthropomorphism. He sees highrise buildings not as phallic symbols, but as metaphors for standing people. (He himself is tall and slim.) This down-with-Freud, up-with-Jung viewpoint is long-established: half a century ago, New York's leading architects attended a Beaux-Arts Costume Ball dressed as their favorite skyscrapers. Pelli even likens the way some of his more horizontal buildings meet the ground to the mythological giant Antaeus, whose strength grew from contact with the earth.

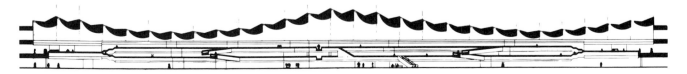

Undulating roof at Fox Hills Mall in Culver City, California, admits an ingenious mixture of direct and reflected daylight.

But the strongest form of that body language is a literal tilt, expressed through asymmetry: an inclination to one side analogous to standing with weight on one foot or an almost anticipatory leaning forward. It is demonstrated to various degrees in the FAA Building, the San Bernardino City Hall, UN City, the Security Pacific Bank, the Winter Garden, and, somewhat less obviously, in the Pacific Design Center and Columbus Commons.

Although subtle, such anthropomorphism nonetheless invites comparison with the values of postmodernism. That expression of discontent with the restrictiveness of standard modernist principles—it is still too diffuse to be called a movement—parallels a growing freedom in Pelli's own work, and its flourishing coincides with a sharp change in the circumstances of his career.

INDEPENDENCE

In 1976, Cesar Pelli could look back upon a highly successful dozen years in Los Angeles, yet that success was not entirely free of paradox. After leaving Eero Saarinen's office he had designed scores of large and complicated buildings, but not a single house, even for himself. His work was well published, but more comprehensively in Japan than in his own country. He had repeatedly produced individualistic and well-regarded projects, but his public identity was linked to first one and then another large firm whose overall professional emphasis was on capabilities other than his strength in design. He had emerged as the best architect of large-scale work in the region, yet the bulk of his major buildings were located hundreds or more often thousands of miles away, while significant local commissions went predominantly to far inferior designers. The Pacific Design Center, his finest piece of local work and arguably the best example of sizable postwar architecture in Southern California, was controversial in a city inured to mediocre design.

Those years had been full of opportunities and creative growth. The laissez-faire intellectual climate and distance from East Coast influences permitted freedom in working

out ideas. DMJM's and Gruen's efficient work-procuring mechanisms had provided a scope and quantity of assignments well beyond what he might have gathered on his own, and those firms' precise division of labor meant that all his time could be devoted to design.

But eventually those advantages began to pale. Work was becoming scarce. Divison of labor meant fragmentation of responsibility and leadership. While ideas had thrived in semi-isolation, further growth might benefit from a new and stimulating milieu. Thus, when offered the position of Dean of Architecture at Yale, Pelli made the difficult decision to move from Los Angeles to New Haven.

In retrospect, the very name of the Connecticut city proved to be an augury, but at the time the move was a professional risk. Pelli was able to count on one commission, as difficult as it was prestigious, for expansion of the Museum of Modern Art. Otherwise he was at a standstill as a practitioner: at one point there was no active work in the office for several months. Pelli had moved to New England only to find a California phenomenon: drought.

When the rains came, they were torrential. In 1979 and 1980, Pelli has had more major projects in hand than at any comparable time with the large Los Angeles firms. He even undertook a commission that would have been too small to consider in Los Angeles: a private residence. But more important than the sudden quantity of work is the evolution that these designs represent. Without the evidence of actual buildings for judgment (none of the current projects will be completed until 1981), it still seems clear that the level of design accomplishment is generally higher than at any previous phase of Pelli's career. Significantly, these projects are not just refinements of earlier thinking and directions: in great part the New Haven work represents fresh thought, creative risk, and emotional enlargement.

Part of this blossoming is due to freedom. For the first time in

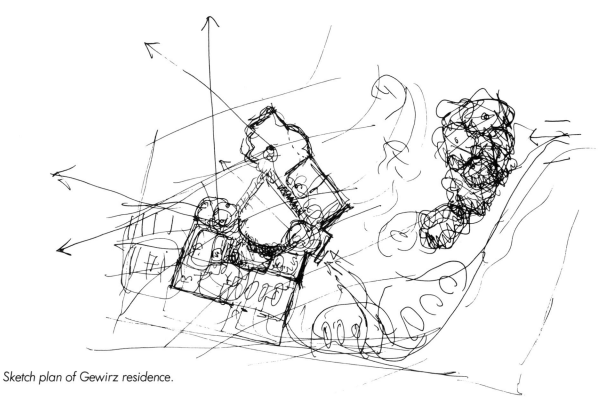

Sketch plan of Gewirz residence.

a 25-year career, Pelli has full design autonomy within the limitations of client decisions, budget, and physical constraints. With his own firm, he is free to set his own priorities and venture into new intellectual territory. Deluged with work and new roles, he says, "I'm having fun."

But another part of that growth can be traced to environment. Pelli has been criticized for insufficient recognition of context in his work. Admittedly, it is not usually a strong suit, but this is typical for high-profile designers in our time, and Pelli is far from being the worst offender. (With the decline of regional practices, this pattern is not unique to him.) Nor is the issue so simple, for he is highly sensitive to the context in which he is based, if not so much to the context of the projects themselves. The real importance of his move to the East lies in Pelli's response to that location.

In Southern California, his work was characteristically free-standing, independent of history, anticipatory of change, machinelike, and enamored of surfaces—in short, it was like Los Angeles itself. These aspects might be softened in projects for other locations, but they remained as basic components of his esthetic and were constantly reinforced by his physical and professional environment.

Pelli's four years in New Haven mark not only a major change of scene but also a recognition of changing architectural times. He now describes himself as a postmodernist, defining the term as any architect whose work comes after modernism.

That wry humor makes a valid point: this catchword need not be the monopoly of designers who use moldings, pediments, colonnades, and other classical elements,

abstracted or literal, in their work. It can also apply, perhaps with greater justification, to architects who have pondered the successes of the modern movement as well as its failures and who use those perceptions to refine the body of 20th-century architectural thought rather than reject it.

Free of overt revisionism, Pelli's new work nevertheless reflects at least one tradition lying outside standard modernism: the great skyscraper style of the 20s and 30s. Most of his new projects are in the shape of towers and make clear homage to that older, "impure" tradition through stepped massing, shaped tops, streamlined curves, decorative spires, vertical notching, or abstracted skyscraper silhouettes incised or laid flat on the sides of his buildings. In these gestures, the emotional tone ranges from a playful rationalism free of irony to a clearly committed romanticism. The subtlest reference to the older skyscrapers lies in the decision to make a Los Angeles tower gradually lighten in color as it ascends. This trick of aerial perspective increases the feeling of height, and was used fifty years ago on skyscrapers in downtown Seattle, on New York's Riverside Drive, and in Niagara Falls, half a block from the Winter Garden site.

Some of this newfound recognition of history and precedent can possibly be traced to internal evolution, but much of it doubtless stems from operating in a historically and physically richer milieu and even more so to regular interchange with metaphorically minded students and the unusually articulate practitioners and theorists who populate the Northeast corridor.

It is still too soon to tell exactly where Pelli's new work will ultimately take him. It is clear, however, that he has been beneficially influenced by his new setting and that his present direction shows a capacity for major nonschismatic change within the modern tradition. Balancing the freedom inherent in postmodernism against some sense of continuity with the older architectural revolution is no easy task, but Cesar Pelli is one of the few who see that middle ground as appealing, just as he is one of the few who have the rational and intuitive capacities to meet such a challenge.

Zigzag profile of proposed Pittsburgh tower renders playful homage to jazz-age architecture.

Projects

Urban Nucleus, Sunset Mountain Park

Fresh from Eero Saarinen's office, Cesar Pelli and his associate Anthony Lumsden quickly gained international recognition for themselves and for DMJM with this splendidly immodest proposal, for mountaintop housing on the fringes of Los Angeles. Equivalent in places to a 60-story building, this efflorescent megastructure is reminiscent of Machu Picchu, the Spanish Steps, and a 1930s film setting of the City of the Future as it should have been done in the first place. In its formal and structural unity, density, mixture of activities, and advantageous use of seemingly unbuildable topography, Sunset Mountain Park compares with, and predates by several years, the "arcologies" of Paolo Soleri. Unlike his utopias, however, it is formally resolved and refined, and was meant to be built, certainly not with ease, but still within the existing social and economic order. In addition to leaving much of the land untouched, it would have allowed the developer to use a difficult site, accommodated the automobile discreetly, and given residents a singular place to live. Not since R.M. Schindler had there been such understanding of the Southern California hillsides, and never before had the problem been solved so deftly at such a heroic scale.

Opposite page: In a bold departure from normal hillside development practice, Cesar Pelli clustered living units around a town center and used the landform to give shape to the building. The upper, central portion of the megastructure would be urban, while the lower, more distant sections would adjoin an untouched mountain landscape.

Above: Partial section through intermediate levels, showing terraced living units, community recreation level, and the inclined elevators that knit the structure together.

Site: An irregularly bounded 3,550-acre (1,440-ha) parcel of rugged undeveloped terrain in the Santa Monica Mountains, zoned for 7,100 residential units.

Design: A megastructure centered on a protruding spur and terracing radially downhill, with one long arm following the line of a connecting ridge. The various terraces contain 1,500 housing units, while the central, topmost portion is the social and commercial core, built above several parking levels. This urban center provides public functions such as a library, school, chapel, post office, bus station, clinic, and theater in addition to stores, offices, restaurants, and a hotel. Inclined elevators link the center with the residential units. Project was not built.

Materials: Reinforced concrete structure throughout.

Client: Sunset International Petroleum Corp.

Teledyne Laboratories

Extending more than 1,000 feet (300 meters), this engineering and laboratory building was Pelli's first opportunity to put his spine principle into practice. Production activities such as assembly and testing were grouped with room for expansion along one side of a passage that Pelli likened to a city street, while support functions such as drafting, administration, and the cafeteria were deployed on the other, facing the front of the site. Most of the workspaces were sheathed in metal, but the corridor was fully glazed and became the prime social and architectural space of the building. Its skin was gently mirrored and cast intriguingly warped reflections in a suburban setting where there was little to reflect. When built, Teledyne embodied the excitement of promising ideas and a new architectural figure, but the refinement of those ideas and the development of that architect's identity awaited later buildings for their fuller expression.

Below: Unrestricted by space, Pelli's first spine building stretches out amidst orange trees on a ¼-mile-square (390-m) tract of land in a former agricultural district. Opposite page: Because its suburban setting provides no architectural context, the building's mirrored skin was designed to reflect itself and abutting wings.

Above: The central third of Teledyne Labs' 800-ft-long (240-m) mirrored corridor stands out against a mountain backdrop in northwestern Los Angeles.
Right: Production spaces at rear of building are sheathed in metal panels.
Opposite page: Viewed from a projecting stair tower, the two-level spine is Teledyne's principal architectural feature as well as its prime public space.

Site: A 35-acre (14-ha) former citrus grove at Corbin Avenue and Nordhoff Street in the Northridge district of the San Fernando Valley. Building: A single-story, 165,000-sq-ft (15,330-sq-m) structure for an aerospace firm, with laboratories, assembly, testing, engineering, and other support functions connected by a two-level spine corridor whose upper portion serves as a visitors' gallery. Roughly half the site is devoted to driveways and parking for 1,950 cars, but portions of the original orange grove have been retained at the periphery. Materials and cost: Steel structural frame, corrugated metal siding, and bronze reflective glass. Cost was $2.85 million in 1968. Client: Teledyne Systems Corp.

Early Skins

In several buildings designed between 1965 and 1970, Pelli emphasized exterior cladding to such a degree that most of their architectural interest was contained in their skins. In part, this was the result of programs and budgets that permitted few expressive opportunities, but it also reflected the architect's determination to explore and develop the esthetic possibilities of enclosing surfaces.

The Century City Medical Plaza is the pioneer, and perhaps also the most extreme, example of this architectural minimalism. Its dark gray skin is as flush and glassy as was technically possible at the time, and its design success essentially resided in its four darkly reflective enclosing planes. In the Toronto-Dominion Bank tower in Vancouver, the same skin system, this time in dark brown, is applied to a more deftly proportioned form, and rather than meeting at right angles, the glass negotiates the corners by means of a bevel. This device, although small and subtle, gave intellectual continuity to the membrane and thus reinforced its symbolic role as a wrapper freed from structural obligations. In addition, cloudier skies and richer urban surroundings than at Century City meant that the reflections in this skin were of a far more satisfying order.

Esthetically, the Federal Building attempted more, but did not entirely conceal its labors. Emphatically sculptured, it attains a degree of polish, yet also shows awkwardness in its beveled curves. By echoing the lines and colors of Airstream trailers and the Graf Zeppelin, this hovering silvery form seems an inadvertent piece of 1930s nostalgia. It is an honest and earnest experiment, but shows how much of Pelli's esthetic hinges on subtleties that escape notice only when successful.

Even though glass is Pelli's favorite medium for enclosing a building, not all the skins were of that material. The Western Electric building in Newark is sheathed in an assortment of flat aluminum panels whose gasketing eliminates the need for a projecting framework of mullions. This versatile system permits individual modules to be virtually all glass, have smaller windows with individual air intakes, or be totally solid to suit predetermined occupancy needs. That arrangement also had nearly twice the thermal effectiveness of a glass curtain wall, but its practical advantages were not fully matched by comparable esthetic ones. No doubt Pelli could have refined this system visually with time, but he decided on a more inventive three-dimensional approach in his later metal walls for the Wells-Fargo and Clorox buildings in Oakland.

The skin carries the major burden of architectural expression in all these buildings. They show how captivating this device can be when used with skill and how far it can advance a project almost unaided. But when compared with Pelli's more multidimensional skin buildings, they also illustrate the limitations of concentrating design effort primarily upon the building's surface.

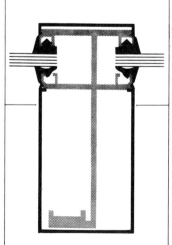

Left: Section through mullion used in Century City Medical Plaza. Most of its depth is contained inside the glass line, permitting a nearly flush exterior surface. Opposite page, right: The Century City Medical Plaza was Pelli's first exercise in the taut skin form. Its four unmodulated rectangular walls are supported by a uniform grid of mullions projecting only ⅜ of an inch (9 mm) beyond the exterior surface.

Below: The form of the Toronto-Dominion Bank Tower is more satisfying than that at Century City, and its curtain wall is more varied and refined. Vision and spandrel panels are of different sizes, paired ventilation recesses appear at midheight, and the corners are delicately chamfered to symbolize the continuity of the skin while adding a subtle element of sculpture to the design.

Left: The Toronto-Dominion Bank Tower reflects the image of an older building and is itself mirrored as a narrow dark band in the convex glass form at left. Sunlight striking the tower's unseen south face is reflected unevenly onto the light wall at center, creating a counterpoint of real and reflected grid lines.

Opposite page: Phantasmagoric mirroring of Hotel Vancouver illustrates an obvious point: the effectiveness of reflective skins is largely dependent on the quality of their surroundings.

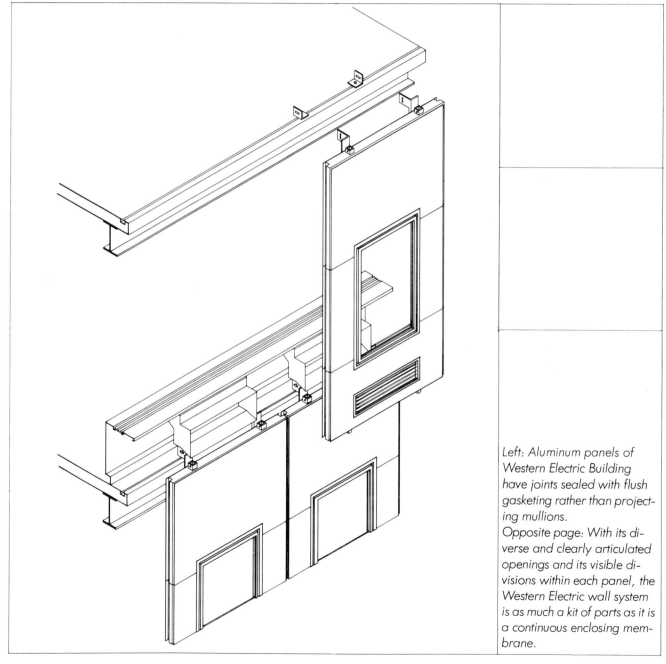

Left: Aluminum panels of Western Electric Building have joints sealed with flush gasketing rather than projecting mullions.
Opposite page: With its diverse and clearly articulated openings and its visible divisions within each panel, the Western Electric wall system is as much a kit of parts as it is a continuous enclosing membrane.

Left: Corner detail of Federal Building reveals the difficulty of producing compound curves within a normal panel system. In later projects Pelli limited curvature to single planes.

Opposite page: Although the Federal Building's highly modeled form is more intriguing than that of a simple prism, the disparity of mirror glass and dull aluminum panels compromises the success of what was intended to be a unified skin.

Century City Medical Plaza: A 17-story tower and adjacent 4-story building, containing a total of 300,000 sq ft (27,870 sq m) of medical office space in a West Los Angeles planned business center, costing $8.2 million in 1969. The skin is dark gray glass with gray anodized aluminum mullions.

Toronto-Dominion Bank Tower: A 30-story, 500,000-sq-ft (46,450-sq-m) office building adjoining a Pelli-designed department store in downtown Vancouver. Both buildings cost $30 million in 1968–1972. The tower skin is bronze tinted glass with bronze anodized mullions.

Federal Building: A 7-story, 214,000-sq-ft (19,880-sq-m) office structure in suburban Hawthorne, Calif., costing $5.3 million in 1973. The skin is silver reflective glass with operable windows and aluminum panels, mullions, and frames.

Western Electric Building: An 18-story, 835,000-sq-ft (77,570-sq-m) office structure in a downtown Newark redevelopment district. The skin is grayish-bronze anodized aluminum and pink reflective glass.

Worldway Postal Center

Within the output of a self-confessed pragmatist, this may be the most pragmatic building of all. The client specified a standard concrete structural system of round columns, conical capitals, and flat floor slabs for the Worldway Postal Center. In the process of exposing this structure, Pelli sliced off the capitals in the plane of the wall to reveal a parabolic edge and filled in the exposed bays with glass, louvered vents, or flush brick as needed, even leaving some open for truck loading. At the rear, a freestanding cage supports a bridge to rooftop parking reached by a bold corkscrew ramp.

The public portion of this immense mail-processing center has an elegance that belies its modest cladding, while the loading docks and rear sections, simply by eliminating glass and substituting brick, display purposeful hardheadedness.

Opposite page: The exposed structural system has a Minoan simplicity and strength.
Below: The building's 32 × 36 ft (10 × 11 m) structural grid is extended to support a bridge to rooftop parking.

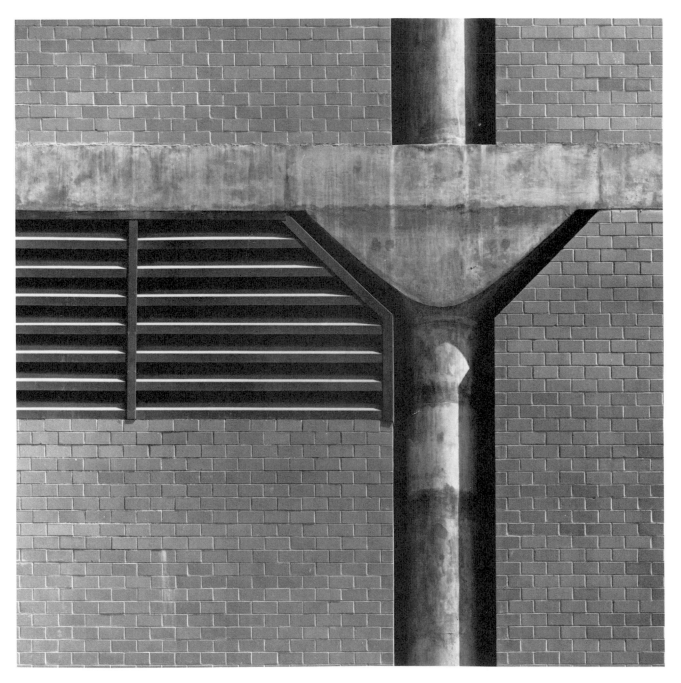

Left: The crisp articulation of frame, glass skin, and brick infill lends distinction to a standardized industrial structure.

Opposite page: Crystalline skin forms sharp contrast with rough concrete structure and brick infill panels.

Site: Approximately 9 acres (4 ha) at Airport and Century Blvds., within the boundaries of Los Angeles International Airport.
Building: A two-story, 390,000-sq-ft (36,230-sq-m) fully mechanized processing center for all air mail and air freight in the Los Angeles region, the first such center in the country. Parking for 460 vehicles is provided on grade and on the building's roof.
Materials and costs: Standard Postal Service structural system for large buildings: reinforced concrete flat slabs, round columns, and conical capitals. This frame is exposed on the exterior and filled with wall panels of brick, brown glass, louvers, or combinations of those materials. Cost was $6.4 million in 1968.
Client: United States Postal Service.

Kukui Gardens

Cesar Pelli is not an architect motivated by overt social concerns, yet it would be difficult to find a better example of urban public housing in the country than Kukui Gardens. Three-fourths of its living units occupy two floors, giving a strong sense of the individual dwelling space. Four apartment blocks, six stories tall, are widely spaced along the edges of the site, but the majority of people live in three-story "townhouses" arranged into short rows that form distinct neighborhoods centered on landscaped pedestrian streets. The carefully judged patterns of public, semiprivate, and private space and the resulting sense of intimacy are all the more remarkable when one considers the more than 800-unit scope of the project.

Striking an understated expressive stance free of both sentimentality and toughness, and produced without political, social, or behavioral science rhetoric, this ensemble suggests that lucid architectural humanism might be the best way of meeting user needs after all.

Below: Housing units are arranged to create a diversity of outdoor spaces that afford both privacy and a street-centered public life.
Opposite page, top: Lowrise modules stack two-story units above ground floor flats and provide each household with exclusive open space.
Opposite page, bottom: Balconies and trellis-shaded decks respond to the Hawaiian climate.

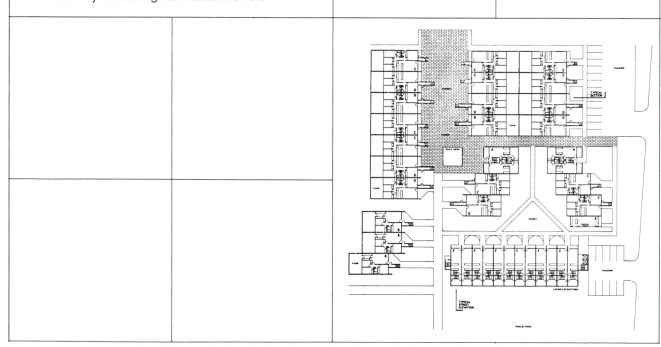

Site: 19.5 acres (8 ha) at Beretania and Liliha Streets, immediately northwest of downtown Honolulu. Its center is a public park.
Buildings: 832 apartments, predominantly of two and three bedrooms, modularly built and combined into two basic arrangements: six-story slabs and three-story rowhouses grouped in a variety of configurations. Automobiles are restricted to the periphery of the site, where 900 parking spaces are provided.
Materials and cost: Concrete block bearing walls and precast concrete floor slabs. Cost was $15 million in 1969.
Client: Clarence T.C. Ching Foundation and the Hawaiian Redevelopment Agency.

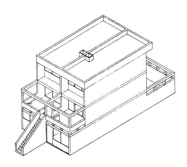

COMSAT Laboratories

"There is really no 'high technology' in architecture," Pelli observes. "What we have is nothing but an expression of high technology." Comprising research, development, and prototype fabrication of communication satellites, COMSAT Laboratories provided an appropriate occasion for the expression, if not the architectural fact, of high technology. That symbolism is conveyed by spine and skin, which are combined with expressive success for the first time in Pelli's work. Compared with Teledyne Labs, the circulation rationale is no longer pure, since a redundant spine parallels the main one outside the laboratory wings, and the aluminum skin is somewhat less elegant in substance than in concept.

Yet both these faults can also be counted as strengths. Redundancy provides broader choice for occupants and corresponds to the back-up systems so essential to complex technological undertakings. And if the skin is marked by plainness and sometimes awkward juxtapositions, this too is in the spirit of a modular building that looks as though it could be dismantled and rearranged, or may even have been several times already. Designed quickly for a client in a rapidly changing field, COMSAT succeeds not in spite of, but because of, its inconsistencies. It is just slick enough to express its high-tech occupancy, yet sufficiently unperfected to represent an industry and an architect in evolution.

Opposite page, top: View of COMSAT Laboratories from freeway at dusk, with porte-cochere at left marking location of spine.
Opposite page, bottom: Detail of secondary corridor. Economy dictated that all curves be faceted in plan, although not in section.
Below: Elevation showing laboratory wings with taller testing area behind and to right.

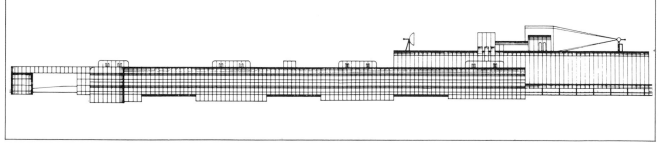

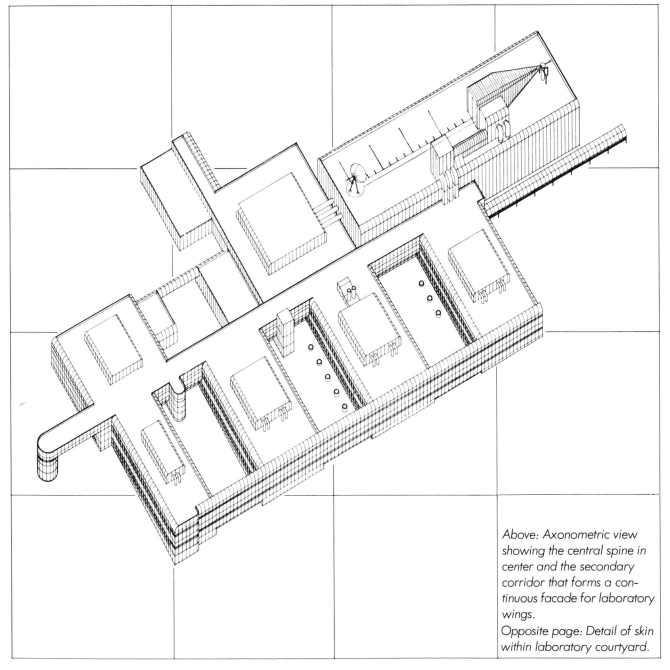

Above: Axonometric view showing the central spine in center and the secondary corridor that forms a continuous facade for laboratory wings.
Opposite page: Detail of skin within laboratory courtyard.

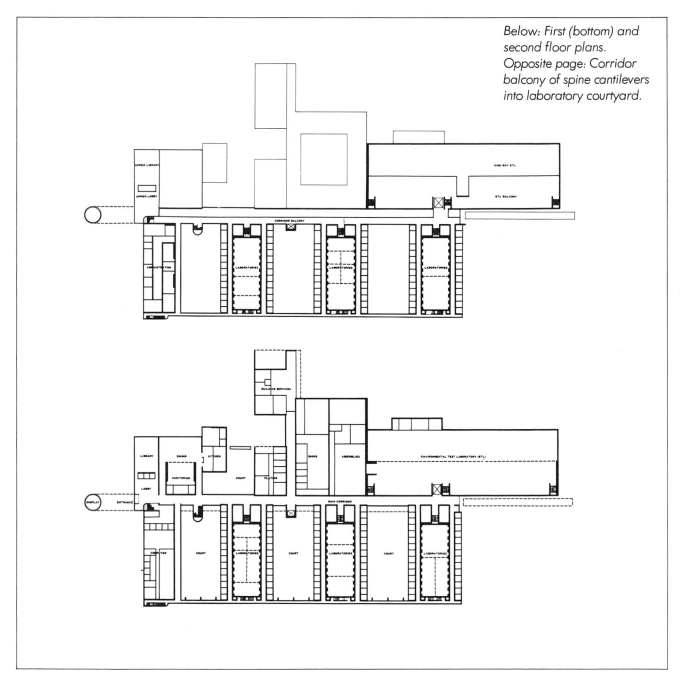

Below: First (bottom) and second floor plans. Opposite page: Corridor balcony of spine cantilevers into laboratory courtyard.

Site: 210 acres (85 ha) of rolling, wooded countryside adjoining Interstate Route 70S, 25 miles (40 km) northwest of Washington, D.C., in Clarksburg, Maryland. Building: 254,000 sq ft (23,600 sq m) of laboratories, administrative and research offices, satellite assembly areas, auditorium, library, and ancillary spaces on two floors plus basement. There is surface parking for 400 cars.
Materials and cost: Steel structural frame, aluminum panels and mullions, clear and bronze tinted glass. The cost, including laboratory facilities, was $9.3 million in 1969.
Client: The Communications Satellite Corp.

San Bernardino City Hall

San Bernardino has long been the butt of Los Angeles humor, but this public building belies the town's unsophisticated reputation. Here Pelli sharpened the forms of the Federal Building and exchanged its mirrored skin for more economical brown glass. The result is a tighter, more boldly sculpted form that marked a clear milestone in the architect's development.

Yet in retrospect the concept seems subtly unrealized and even a bit flatfooted. The City Hall is intellectually impressive but viscerally just off the mark. Its newly built neighbors are not visually supportive and its intended companion piece, a large theater designed by Pelli, has not been built. And although he is generally correct in preferring dark glass to mirrored, in this case one suspects that the City Hall's precisely chiseled volume and generous soffit would have been better expressed if wrapped in silver.

Opposite page: Set in sparse surroundings, the dark brown reflective skin of the San Bernardino City Hall springs to life in cloudy weather.
Below: The stepped plaza surrounding the building was also designed as a forecourt between the City Hall (center) and a Civic Theater (top) that has not been built.

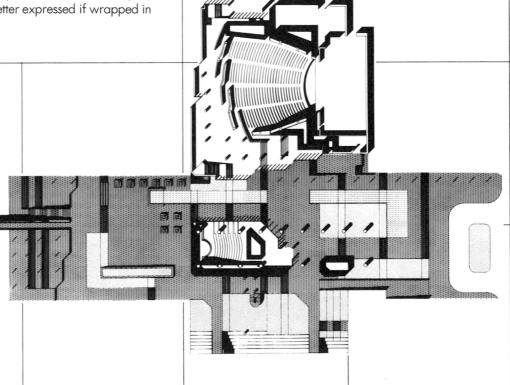

Left: Seen from the plaza's upper end, the uninflected rear face conveys a rather somber character.
Opposite page, top: At night the skin dissolves to reveal the pattern of offices within.
Opposite page, bottom: The building's dynamic aspect is most apparent from the northeast.

Site: A 2.3-acre (0.9-ha) parcel within a superblock that forms part of a 93-acre (38-ha) downtown redevelopment district. The building occupies the vacated right of way of Third Street between D and E Streets, and its western plaza is connected to an enclosed shopping mall by a pedestrian bridge.

Building: A six-story, 112,500-sq-ft (10,450-sq-m) structure housing all city administrative offices and the council chamber. A 32,000-sq-ft (2,970-sq-m) exhibit hall is located beneath the western plaza, and a series of terraces descends from there to ground level at the eastern end of the site. A 1,100 car parking structure adjoins the city hall's landscaped grounds to the south, and a civic theater was originally planned to the north.

Materials and costs: Reinforced concrete columns, beams, slabs, and shear walls; bronze tinted glass windows and dark bronze opaque glass spandrels. Cost, including exhibit hall, was $4.95 million in 1972. Client: City of San Bernardino.

UN City, Vienna

Here Pelli's ideas of deriving building form from circulation and growth are carried to their peak. Not only is there a linear spine that anchors the UN City scheme in plan, but flights of escalators and highrise elevator banks extend the concept into three dimensions, unlike Pelli's earlier ground-hugging laboratory buildings. The strategies for expansion similarly capitalize upon the vertical as well as the horizontal. But what makes the scheme remarkable is not its deftness of organization so much as the architectural clarity and resolution of its expression. The three main elements of spine, assembly spaces, and office towers are brought together with a calculated tension that allows each part to retain its identity and yet contribute to a ramified whole. This may be an unintended metaphor of national self-interest versus the possibilities of international discourse.

The spine and tower forms and their articulation recall James Stirling, and have undergone further metamorphosis in such projects of Pelli's as the Niagara Falls Winter Garden and the unbuilt Crossroads Galleria in Los Angeles. It has influenced the work of other architects as well: its most literal descendant, the Dallas Hyatt Regency, adapts its form but not its organization.

Conceived on a huge scale—the spine is over 1,500 feet (460 meters) long and one tower rises nearly 600 feet (180 meters)—UN City has a monumentality appropriate to its size and symbolic importance. In its discipline of concept, accommodation of growth, and tough-minded romanticism, this project vies strongly for preeminence among Pelli's works. The design won first prize in an international competition that drew 280 entries from 50 countries, but Viennese intrigue blocked its construction and substituted a lesser design of local origin. Had it been built, and assuming the further design development that actual construction would demand, this might well have become one of the textbook examples of 20th-century architecture.

Left: Trusswork of assembly hall structure extends into space of main circulation concourse.
Opposite page: View from east with existing television tower at right. Assembly halls in foreground would be supported by lattice frame trusses and would project over a small lake.

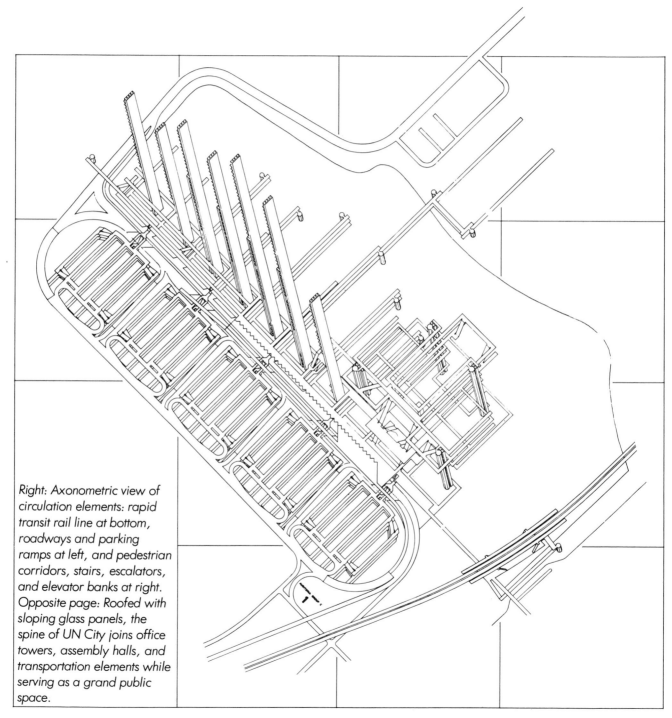

Right: Axonometric view of circulation elements: *rapid transit rail line at bottom, roadways and parking ramps at left, and pedestrian corridors, stairs, escalators, and elevator banks at right. Opposite page: Roofed with sloping glass panels, the spine of UN City joins office towers, assembly halls, and transportation elements while serving as a grand public space.*

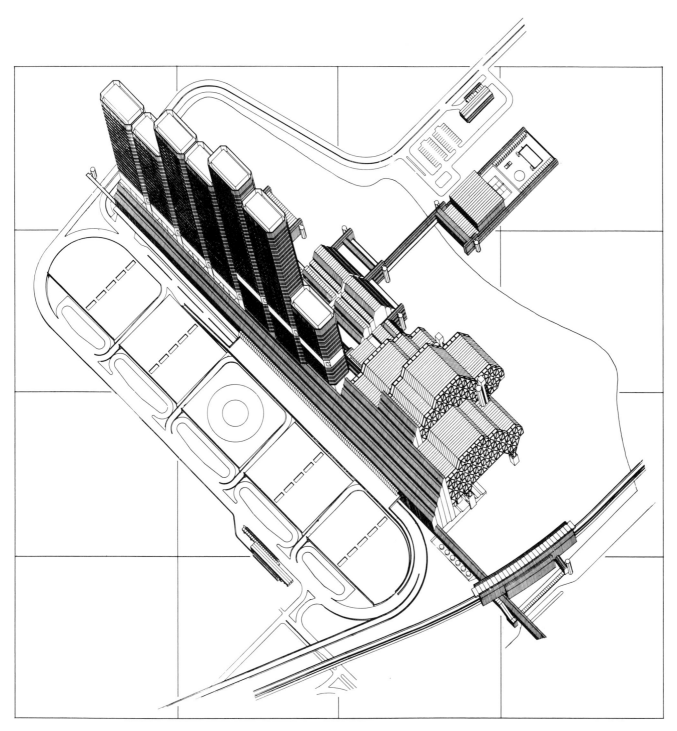

Above: View of UN City from west.
Opposite page: Elevations. The office towers would rise free of the spine and lower service wings, supported by twin concrete cores and two-story deep trusses expressed as light-colored exterior bands.

Site: A large park between the old and new channels of the Danube River, immediately northwest of the Wagramer Strasse and 2.5 miles (4 km) northeast from the center of the old city. An elevated rapid transit line would serve the site from the south.

Building: Offices for six international organizations and 15 conference and assembly halls of various sizes within a structure of 4 million sq ft (371,610 sq m). Designed as a series of 10 modular elements attached to a connecting spine, the project lends itself to incremental expan-

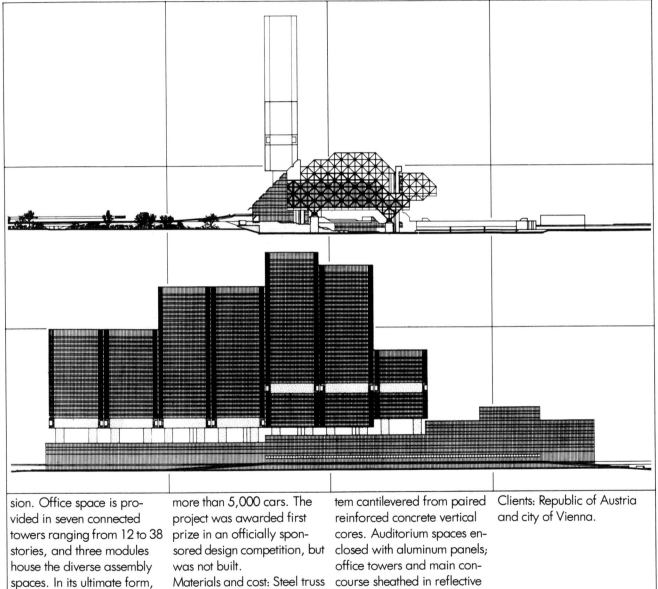

sion. Office space is provided in seven connected towers ranging from 12 to 38 stories, and three modules house the diverse assembly spaces. In its ultimate form, the building would serve a daytime population of 25,000 workers and 5,000 visitors and accommodate more than 5,000 cars. The project was awarded first prize in an officially sponsored design competition, but was not built.

Materials and cost: Steel truss structure in conference center and in main concourse. Office floors supported by two-way Vierendeel truss system cantilevered from paired reinforced concrete vertical cores. Auditorium spaces enclosed with aluminum panels; office towers and main concourse sheathed in reflective glass supported on aluminum mullions. The entire project was budgeted at $150 million in 1969.

Clients: Republic of Austria and city of Vienna.

Commons and Courthouse Center

Essentially an indoor town square for America's most architecturally advantaged small city, the Commons and Courthouse Center is a publicly owned space fronting on the main downtown street of Columbus, Indiana, and attached to a much larger private shopping center. Its uses range from casual time-passing to large organized events, and its ability to provoke and serve a diversity of goings-on has made it a popular success. In its program, it is Pelli's most overt social space, and in its execution it is his most heterogeneously well-used.

But if the building is a generous host, so is it a somewhat awkward guest. It sits unabashedly modern on Victorian Washington Street, a single volume of glass amid intricate masonry, dark and monochromatic in a field of variegated color. Good intentions were not lacking: roof lines were related to those of neighbors, the ground floor was elaborately indented in quest of the scale and spirit of the older storefronts, and, as usual, the skin was devised to reflect its surroundings. But the issue was one of material as well as geometry. Whatever its concessions to local form, the glass membrane is inherently at odds with the spirit, tactile quality, and multiformity of the Victorian environment.

After sundown, however, these outward differences lose their importance, for the skin dissolves and the interior clearly comes on display. Then the Commons' essence as a social vehicle becomes not only visible from the street, but dominant over the external architecture, and the town square is manifest as structured light and space.

Opposite page: Faceted bronze glass skin reflects the forms of a previous century. Below: Although its glass skin contrasts strongly with the masonry facades of its Victorian neighbors, roof and soffit heights were chosen to align with those prevailing on Washington Street.

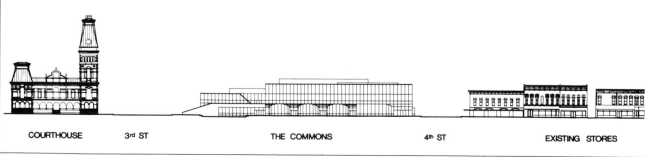

COURTHOUSE   3rd ST   THE COMMONS   4th ST   EXISTING STORES

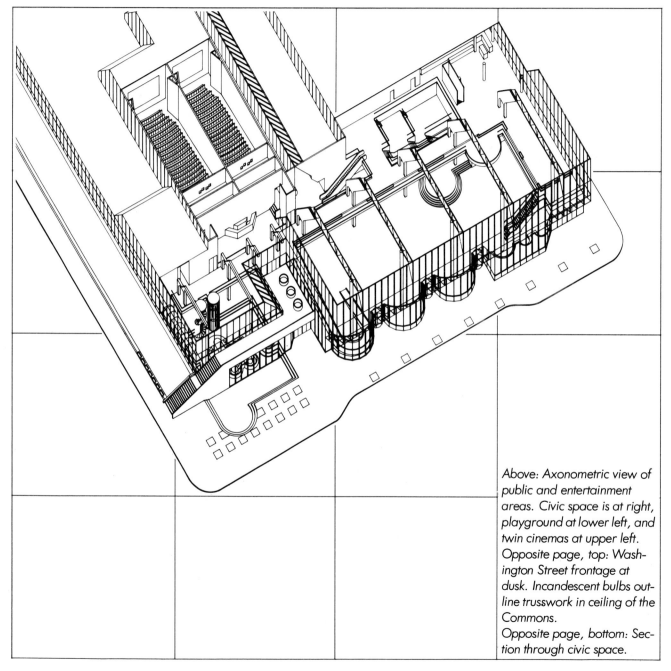

Above: Axonometric view of public and entertainment areas. Civic space is at right, playground at lower left, and twin cinemas at upper left.
Opposite page, top: Washington Street frontage at dusk. Incandescent bulbs outline trusswork in ceiling of the Commons.
Opposite page, bottom: Section through civic space.

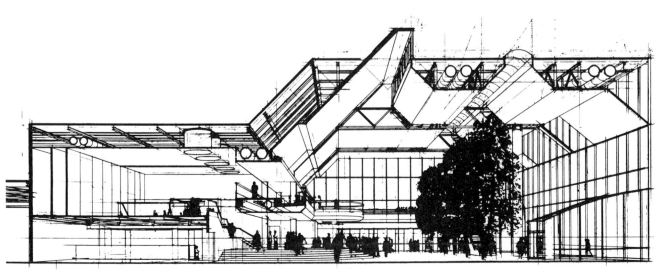

Above: View from mezzanine showing Jean Tinguely's kinetic sculpture, Chaos I.
Right: Annotated floor plan indicates the range of activities that occur in the Commons.

Opposite page: Shopping mall of the Courthouse Center is lit by a shed-roof skylight that takes on an apparent gable form when reflected by an adjacent mirrored wall.

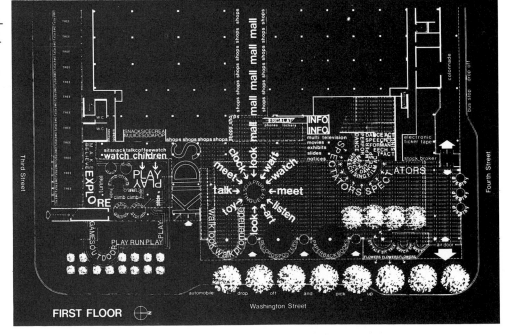

FIRST FLOOR

Site: 11.9 acres (4.8 ha) fronting on Washington Street, the main downtown thoroughfare, adjacent to the Victorian county courthouse. The building occupies two blocks and parking takes up three more in Columbus, Indiana.

Building: The project comprises two distinct legal entities. The Commons is a city-owned space of 63,000 sq ft (5,850 sq m) occupying two levels and encompassing a playground, sitting areas, exhibition gallery, performing stage, snack bar, and cafeteria. The Courthouse Center is a 180,000-sq-ft (16,720-sq-m) privately operated shopping center with ground and mezzanine floors accommodating a Sears department store, a twin cinema, and other retail and service establishments.

Materials and cost: Steel frame structure throughout, with exposed trusses in Commons. Exterior skin is bronze-toned glass. Cost was between $26 and $31 per square foot or approximately $7 million in 1973. Clients: City of Columbus and Irwin Management Co., Inc.

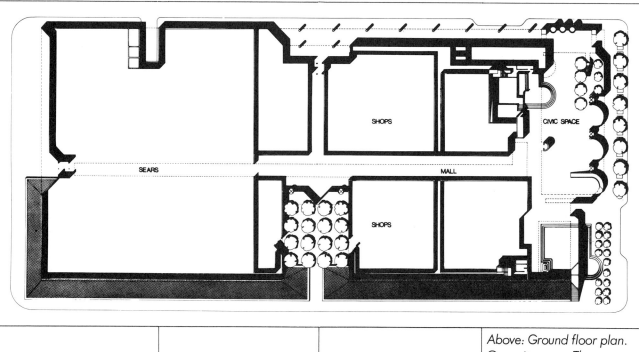

SHOPS

CIVIC SPACE

SEARS

MALL

SHOPS

Above: Ground floor plan. Opposite page: The essence of the Commons and Courthouse Center lies in its heavily used public space fronting on the main street of downtown Columbus.

At once intimate and spatially generous, the subtly colored interior of the Security Pacific National Bank is unique among Pelli's works.

Security Pacific National Bank

Taking up about 2 percent of a San Bernardino block, this little building is one of pleasant surprises. Its exterior, despite a quirky silhouette, is a bit forbidding since it lacks windows on its street faces. Inside, however, Security Pacific National Bank is a naturally lit single space, four stories tall and flanked by balcony offices. Its height and sweeping lines are potentially monumental, but its scale is intimate and those divergent tendencies manage to coexist surprisingly well. North light is diffused through a tall window wall that runs the full length of the structure, and the other walls glow in a softly graded color scheme depicting the hues of a sunset sky. Outside, bluish-gray and dull orange tiled walls also play on that theme, and densely spaced rows of palms lend so strong an air of oasis to the drive-in teller lanes that one's pleasure outweighs any ironic thoughts about the exaltation of the automobile in California culture. Of all Pelli's completed buildings, this seems deservedly the one most likely to inspire affection.

Security Pacific National Bank devotes most of its downtown site to parking and drive-though banking services, but is also generously planted with 150 pine, palm, camphor, and pear trees and twice that number of smaller plants.

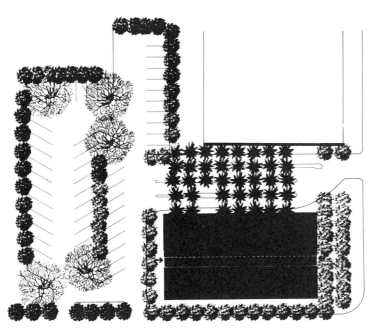

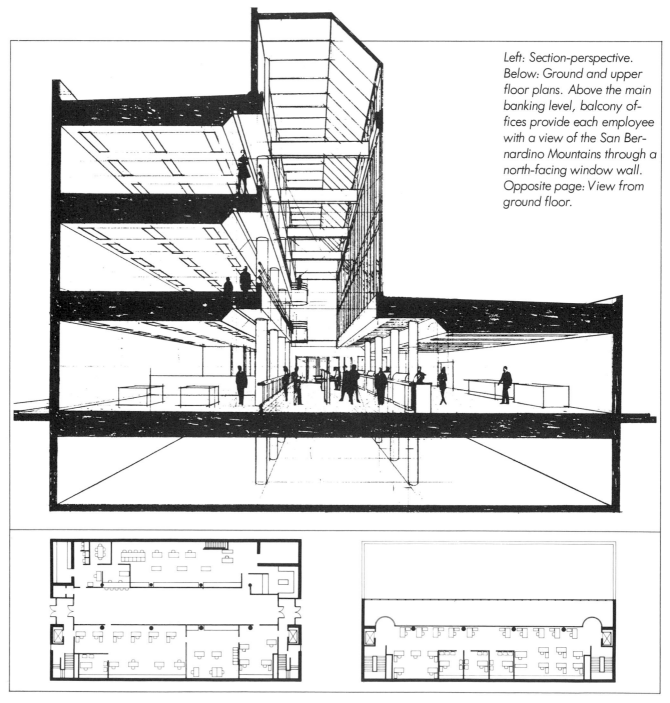

Left: Section-perspective. Below: Ground and upper floor plans. Above the main banking level, balcony offices provide each employee with a view of the San Bernardino Mountains through a north-facing window wall. Opposite page: View from ground floor.

Site: An irregularly shaped parcel of 0.85 acres (0.3 ha) at the corner of 4th and D Streets in downtown San Bernardino, California.
Building: A three-story, 25,500-sq-ft (2,370-sq-m) structure with public banking services on the ground level, regional administrative offices above, and support functions in the basement. There are four drive-through teller's lanes and parking spaces for 50 cars.
Materials and cost: Reinforced concrete frame, glazed Norman brick, and bronze-tinted glass. Cost was $968,000 in 1972.
Client: Security Pacific National Bank.

Oakland City Center

In its responsiveness to climate and city form as well as in its visual sophistication, the curtain wall system on these paired office buildings of the Oakland City Center represents one of Pelli's strongest accomplishments in a favorite medium. Metal panels scooped inward but otherwise flush with the window plane produce strong shadow patterns when sunlit, while allowing unhampered window reflectivity when shaded. These spandrels assume three sizes: narrow at corners and north walls, wider on walls facing east and west, and wider still on the south. The proportion of vision glass to insulated wall is thus varied in step with the solar heat load, and facades are given an intriguing differentiation. By boldly chamfering all corners and setting the Clorox tower on a 45-degree skew to the

Wells-Fargo Building, Pelli has not only maximized views but also echoed two diagonal streets that radiate from Broadway immediately to the north and allowed each structure to reflect the other. Those walls also yield sliced images of several old masonry buildings, and the beige spandrel color shows subtle cognizance of their presence.

One aspect of this ingenious cladding is questionable: the deep spandrel indentations, although purely formal devices for casting shadows, take on the functional look of ventilation intakes. This small anomaly aside, the Oakland City Center is an economically modest yet quietly brilliant response to the questions of energy, context, and the nature of the wall itself.

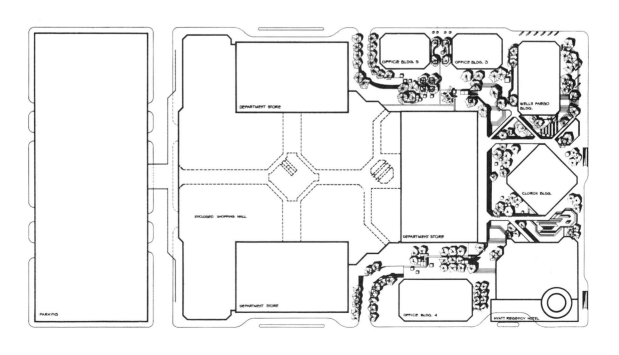

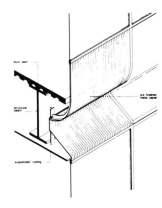

*Opposite page: Site plan
Right: The Clorox Tower's diagonal placement to the Wells Fargo Building on right allows proximity while maintaining views from both structures. By varying the height of window heads and sills, Pelli produced three different proportions of glass (darker bands) to spandrels in response to solar orientation. As preferred office locations, however, all corners have maximum glass area regardless of position.
Above: Isometric section through Wells Fargo wall showing construction of indented spandrel.
Following pages:
Page 74: Oakland City Hall reflected in Wells Fargo skin.
Page 75: Wells Fargo Building corner.*

Site: An irregular portion of a superblock within a downtown urban renewal district. The buildings front upon Broadway between 12th and 14th Streets and are connected to a major BART subway station.

Buildings: The Wells Fargo Building is 10 stories tall and contains 242,000 sq ft (22,480 sq m) of office space, with stores, a bank, and restaurants on the ground and subterranean levels. The Clorox Building is 24 stories tall and contains approx 485,000 sq ft (45,060 sq m) of offices and lower-floor commercial uses similar to Wells Fargo.

Materials and cost: Steel frame structure, bronze-tinted glass, embossed sheet metal spandrel panels (steel in Wells Fargo, aluminum in Clorox). Wells Fargo was built for $9.2 million in 1973 and Clorox for approximately $20 million in 1975.

Client: Grubb & Ellis Company.

Winter Garden & Rainbow Center Mall

Pelli has long been interested in plate tectonics, the study of large-scale shifts in the earth's crust, and in its upwardly shearing thrust, the Winter Garden seems to manifest some powerful geologic force. Derived in shape from UN City's main hall, its structure is not just expressed, but reveled in: the pattern of red-painted trusses, cross-bracing, gusset plates, tie rods, and window framing achieves an almost Victorian busyness that is both wonderful to behold and unmatched in Pelli's normally smooth-surfaced output. Yet for all its visual dynamism and articulation of parts, this space-age conservatory is not quite what it appears to be in photographs. It feels more intimate in the flesh than its heroic imagery and 155-by-175-foot (47-by-53-meter) dimensions lead one to expect. Nor is it quite as strong an experience of space and light as one would think: dense greenery, raised walkways and platforms, and massive concrete columns fill the space and domesticate its nascent grandeur, and sitting under frequently overcast skies, the nearly all-glass enclosure admits light of such omnipresence that it lacks the drama that more shadow and contrast would produce.

In compensation for these mild disappointments, there is an uncanny feeling of contained volume when seen from outside. This is underscored at night, when the inside space appears tangibly distinct as though it were filled with a clear yet thickly refractive liquid or even carved from a huge block of crystal and magically filled with red filigree.

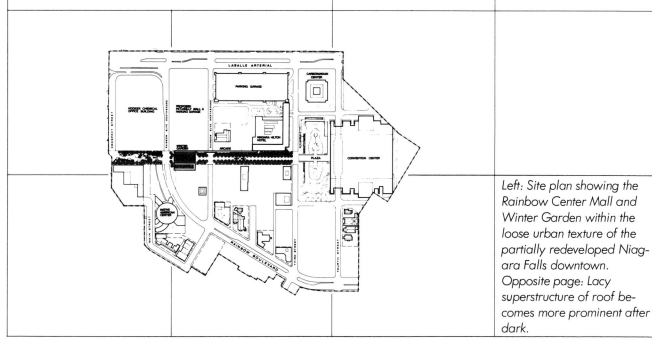

Left: Site plan showing the Rainbow Center Mall and Winter Garden within the loose urban texture of the partially redeveloped Niagara Falls downtown. Opposite page: Lacy superstructure of roof becomes more prominent after dark.

Above: Winter Garden and Mall on an overcast fall day. Intended as a tourist destination point and downtown commercial focus, the Winter Garden and its adjoining two-level concourse at right also soften the winter rigors of a northern climate. Opposite page: At lower levels, Winter Garden's space is filled with columns, raised walkways, and exotic foliage. Effectively that of a greenhouse, the structure was designed to admit maximum natural light.

78

Site: A 1,500-ft-long (450-m), 100-ft-wide (30-m) strip linking the convention center to a riverfront park in downtown Niagara Falls. Lying within an 82-acre (33-ha) downtown redevelopment district, the site is bor·dered by vacant land and a few widely spaced buildings.

Building: An indoor garden and pedestrian destination point of approximately 30,000 sq ft (2,790 sq m) densely planted and flanked by balconies intended to connect with future commercial buildings. A two-level enclosed walkway extends approximately 500 ft (150 m) to a new hotel, running parallel to the axis of the outdoor pedestrian mall.

Materials and cost: Exposed structural steel frame, clear and laminated glass, and aluminum curtain wall framing. Cost was $7.9 million for the structures and the mall in 1977.

Client: Niagara Falls Urban Renewal Agency.

Pacific Design Center

Pelli's Los Angeles landmark, the Pacific Design Center is an ultramarine leviathan rising from a sea of little houses. Its popular nickname of the Blue Whale indicates its ambiguous yet undeniable place in the public consciousness. Essentially windowless, this vitreous extrusion is the result of disparate floor areas devoted to various interior furnishing category showrooms and Pelli's resolve to create an unmistakable identity. Since most of the skin is opaque, its reflectivity is strong, and since its form is highly modeled, the reflections have unusual richness. Inside, the building has an impressive variety of spaces, including corridors that wander like medieval streets, a grand barrel-vaulted galleria on top, and a remarkable escalator stack suspended within a cylindrical void. Here is a speculative undertaking that manages to outshine the city's recent public monuments, but its quirky form and sharp break in scale have puzzled and even outraged many Los Angeles residents. Its contextual effects may be honestly debated today, but in time the sea will rise, surely enough to make it seem more like a dolphin.

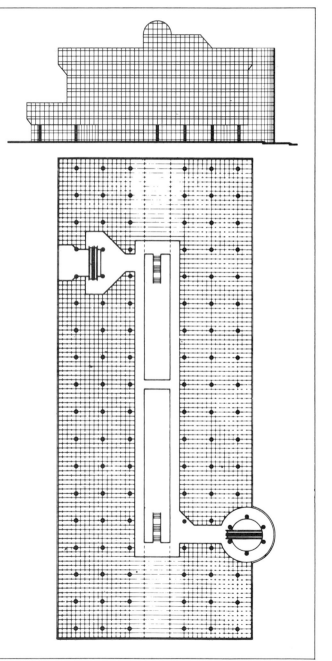

Opposite page, top: San Vicente Blvd. elevation. Due to unusually lofty top and bottom floors, this six-story building is as tall as a typical 14-story apartment building. Opposite page, bottom: Sixth floor plan. Escalators at diagonally opposite ends of the building are linked by a formal galleria on the two topmost floors and by meandering corridors at lower levels (see page 17). Despite this free treatment of circulation space, the planning conforms to a 5-ft (1.5-m) module and, excepting the northernmost bay, to a 30-ft (9-m) square column grid. Left: View along Melrose Avenue frontage. Reflection transforms the semicircular escalator projection into an apparent full cylinder, an illusion which is most convincing at night.

Above: Rear view.
Right: Front escalator bank spans a six-story cylindrical void, half within the main building volume and half projecting beyond.
Opposite page: Extending 530 ft (160 m) and reaching a height of 60 ft (18 m), the Pacific Design Center galleria is a grand space akin to the railroad stations that flourished two generations ago.

Left: Flat expanse of Los Angeles is mirrored in upper-floor skin, while inclined facet reflects Melrose Avenue below.
Opposite page: An oddly shaped extrusion wrapped in a glistening skin of rich blue, the Pacific Design Center has inspired both admiration and dislike among Los Angeles residents.

Site: 16 acres (6 ha) of gently sloping land fronting on Melrose Avenue and San Vicente Blvd. The surrounding West Hollywood neighborhood is, by Los Angeles standards, old, densely settled, and diverse in its activities. It is something of a residential bohemia as well as the center of the region's interior design and high-style furniture industries.

Building: A six-story, 750,000-sq-ft (69,680-sq-m) furniture mart and design showplace, with stores and eating places in the ground level and exhibit space, assembly rooms, and a private club in various portions of the building. Over half the site is devoted to surface parking for 1,150 cars.

Materials and cost: Steel structural frame, opaque blue spandrel glass, bronze-tinted vision glass, and structural gasketing on an aluminum frame. Cost was approximately $20 million in 1975.

Client: Sequoia Pacific, a division of Southern Pacific Co.

United States Embassy, Tokyo

Limitations abounded in this design for America's third-largest embassy. The State Department mandated the building's width and corridor position, conservative earthquake safety codes dictated a staunch structure, and the desire to keep a prominent site as open as possible led to an eccentric building placement. The result is largely a thing of skin and bones: thin scored concrete panels and operable mirror glass combine elegantly in a finely crafted flush curtain wall, while the overscaled concrete framework dominates the building's short ends and forms an impressive entrance loggia along one side. Indoors, the structure is no less prominent, with its robust columns exposed inside offices and marching in pairs down the corridors.

The extreme linearity of this scheme — each wing is nearly seven times longer than it is wide — suggests the presence of a classic Pelli spine, and although site boundaries and stairs at each end preclude extension, the embassy nevertheless appears poised for growth. Or, alternatively, it looks as though each wing were sliced to size from a far longer stock and then the cut ends carefully finished with banded concrete closures. Sited on line with its main approach avenue but at an oblique angle, the embassy inflects space and vision gracefully in a crowded and chaotic city.

This building impressed the officers of a Korean insurance company so strongly that they requested an identical curtain wall for their new home office. The floor plan and structural proportions are changed, most of the enlivening irregularities have been homogenized, a tile finish has replaced the concrete panel facing, and a lofty greenhouse has been added at the lobby, but otherwise the Daehan Kyoyuk Life Insurance Company is the Tokyo Embassy's Seoul brother.

Opposite page: Impeccably crafted concrete and mirrored window bands, unified by an overriding rectangular grid, produce a building enclosure of unusual elegance. Below: Entrance level plan. The structural frame is left open to form the lobby and portico.

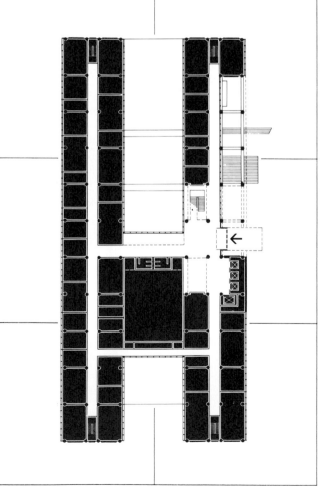

Above: Garden court lies between tall and low wings.

Left: Exposed structural frame within entrance portico. The embassy's careful detailing is supported by an extraordinary level of construction skill.

Opposite page, top: View from northeast. Lower wing can be expanded by adding a fourth floor.

Opposite page, bottom: The stepped roof line echoes a sloping site, and the elevator banks are manifest as a windowless vertical stripe.

Left: *Daehan Kyoyuk Life Insurance Company uses the design elements of the embassy, but in a far more regularized and static manner.*
Below: *Rear of Daehan Kyoyuk Life Insurance Company headquarters is graced by an enclosed tropical garden that combines the form of the Pacific Design Center galleria with the content of the Niagara Falls Winter Garden.*
Opposite page, above: *East elevation. Building is indented on lower floors to form a tall entrance portico framed by the exposed structural grid.*
Opposite page, below: *Axonometric view of lower floors of main wing. Windowless portion of long wall marks location of elevators.*

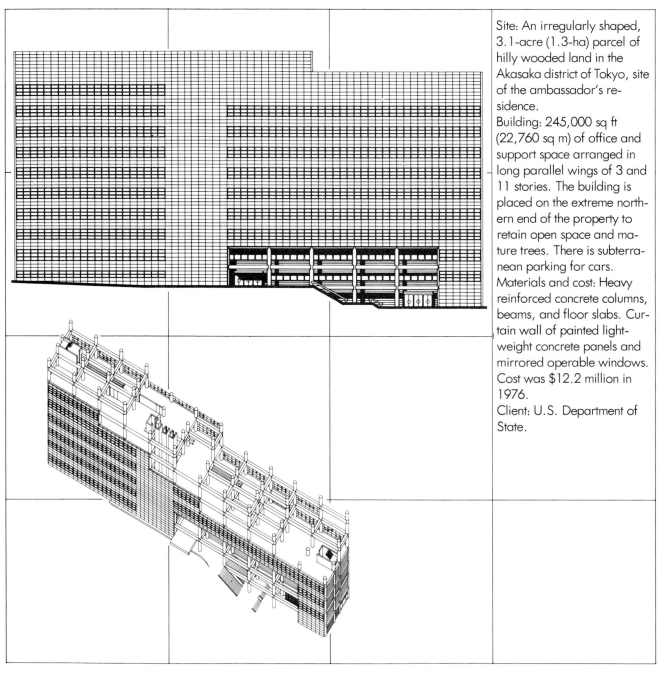

Site: An irregularly shaped, 3.1-acre (1.3-ha) parcel of hilly wooded land in the Akasaka district of Tokyo, site of the ambassador's residence.

Building: 245,000 sq ft (22,760 sq m) of office and support space arranged in long parallel wings of 3 and 11 stories. The building is placed on the extreme northern end of the property to retain open space and mature trees. There is subterranean parking for cars.

Materials and cost: Heavy reinforced concrete columns, beams, and floor slabs. Curtain wall of painted lightweight concrete panels and mirrored operable windows. Cost was $12.2 million in 1976.

Client: U.S. Department of State.

Recent Towers

New work came into Pelli's office in 1979 with surprising suddenness, and to an overwhelming degree those new commissions were for highrise buildings. The design response was no less surprising, since each of these towers departs in one respect or another from the earlier Pelli paradigm for that building type. Crisp, vertically extruded prisms with flat tops and generally uniform skins no longer appear in pure form, but are modified by devices that flourished a half-century ago: stepped setbacks, sculpted tops, streamlined corners, individually expressed windows, and even ornamental spires. In some schemes, the abstracted profile of an older-style skyscraper is carved out of a tower's volume or appears as an inlaid silhouette defined by a change of color or material.

At times, alternative designs were not worked out beyond rough sketches, and three of the projects will definitely not be built. But even if this homage to older forms and styles is not always fully developed or assured of realization, its sudden and vigorous emergence is nonetheless welcome. In no other comparably brief period of Pelli's career has there been so much uninhibited experiment and such a sense of playfulness and romanticism. This freedom is expressed not only in the designs, but in the soft and sketchy presentation methods as well. Those techniques are reminiscent of the charcoal drawings of Hugh Ferriss, just as aspects of the designs recall the buildings that he rendered so dramatically in the 20s and 30s.

Yet for all their reference to times and styles past, these are not historicist buildings in the sense of Philip Johnson's "Chippendale Skyscraper" for AT&T. They deal with the spirit of older skyscraper styles rather than appropriating their forms and details. (The final Pittsburgh scheme is a possible exception.) Rather than quoting the past, Pelli is excerpting and paraphrasing it in such a way that the momentum of his development is not interrupted and our sense of the present is not under assault.

Right: The chiseled, crystalline tops of the Four Leaf Towers and the octogonal transition they make to the main structure recall a fifty-year-old visionary drawing of Hugh Ferriss, "Night in the Science Zone" (below). Opposite page: Proposed Pittsburgh tower's zigzag profile and telescoping central silhouette render playful homage to jazz-age architecture.

Asked to give emphasis to the corner of a Denver site, Pelli did so through both setbacks and a change of material that reiterated the zigzag form of this proposed tower.

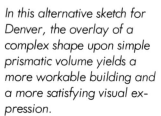

In this alternative sketch for Denver, the overlay of a complex shape upon simple prismatic volume yields a more workable building and a more satisfying visual expression.

*Above: This early study for
900 Third Avenue was a gen-
tle essay in the Streamlined
Modern mode.
Above right: Final version of
900 Third Avenue represents
a more complex massing
combined with a shallow
layering of zigzag forms.*

The Bunker Hill tower's stepped corner elements each seem to be half of a classic Depression-era skyscraper. Similarly, its recessed portion is the negative volume of a prototypical older tower turned upside down. Coexisting with these references to the past is a serious, refined, and thoroughly elegant sculptural form that makes no effort to deny its modern origins.

Left, top and bottom: Initial studies for the Oliver Tyrone III project in Pittsburgh concentrated upon abstractly stepped profiles, cool, detached symbolism, and parity with nearby structures. Opposite page: The entry to the Second Chicago Tribune Tower Competition, perhaps because it was an abstract exercise with no possibility of realization, lacks the vigor of the other tower designs and instead conveys a somber anonymous presence.

Bunker Hill Office Tower: A 62-story, 1.8 million-sq-ft (167,225-sq-m) office structure designed as part of a larger proposal submitted for consideration to the Los Angeles Community Redevelopment Agency. The skin is honed granite, reflective and clear glass.

Oliver Tyrone III: Unexecuted proposals for a downtown Pittsburgh office building of 34 stories, clad in tinted and mirrored glass. The final proposal, also unexecuted, was for a considerably taller building in unspecified materials. (Shown on page 22.)

Chicago Tribune Tower Competition: A 44-story, granite and glass skin submission to the 1980 reincarnation of the classic 1922 international competition.

Denver Tower: Sketches for a tentative project clad in mirrored and tinted glass.

Four Leaf Towers: Twin 41-story residential building of 200 living units each, located in suburban Houston, clad in tinted and opaque glass in four colors, and budgeted at $66 million in 1980.

900 Third Avenue: A 35-story, 448,000-sq-ft (41,620-sq-m) office tower at 3rd Avenue and 54th Street in Manhattan, budgeted at $38 million in 1980.

Biennale House

Although steeped in pragmatism, Pelli is not trapped in it. Invited to solve a problem outside reality, he became a raconteur as well as an architect, making up a narrative to fit his design and vice versa. Within this hybrid art form, we are shown the growth of a building, a succession of social forms, the spread of a city, and the displacement of pure enjoyment by purposeful occupancy.

Yet for all its verbal dimension the Biennale House is still primarily the product of architectural imagination displayed through the poetic interplay of opposed parts. The literary conceit and geometric artifact are one, but the latter is more highly developed. Its reinforced concrete spine is permanent, but will become chipped and stained with age. The glass walls are temporary, but will remain unchanged and unblemished as long as they exist. On one side of the spine they are tinted in various colors. On the other they gradually range from transparency to strong mirrorization, an effect first exploited by Los Angeles artist Larry Bell. Between and around these walls trees grow, cars proliferate, and people come and go. The house encourages its imagined occupants to complete it, and it invites its real audience to supply referents for its strong yet unspecific symbolism.

Do its various states represent the ages of humankind? Does the progression from hedonism to domestic use and from private visitation to communal living constitute a metaphor of societal development? Is the undying concrete spine paradoxically symbolic of the masonry esthetic that Pelli deems obsolete? Does the dismantling of the exquisite glass walls foreshadow a future change in attitude toward the architect's favorite material? The questions are plentiful, the answers myriad. And yet, given the nature of the assignment, is not this fanciful product a most pragmatic solution?

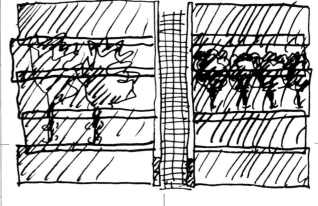

Below: Cesar Pelli's sketch for the house in its first metamorphosis. Mirrored glass walls are at left, concrete spine at center, and tinted glass walls at right. Trees grow in spaces defined by the walls.

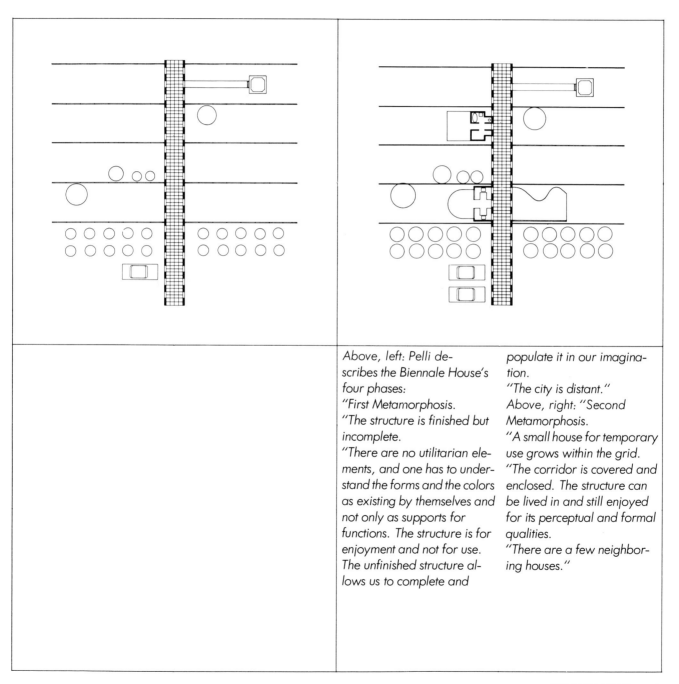

Above, left: Pelli describes the Biennale House's four phases:
"First Metamorphosis.
"The structure is finished but incomplete.
"There are no utilitarian elements, and one has to understand the forms and the colors as existing by themselves and not only as supports for functions. The structure is for enjoyment and not for use. The unfinished structure allows us to complete and

populate it in our imagination.
"The city is distant."
Above, right: "Second Metamorphosis.
"A small house for temporary use grows within the grid.
"The corridor is covered and enclosed. The structure can be lived in and still enjoyed for its perceptual and formal qualities.
"There are a few neighboring houses."

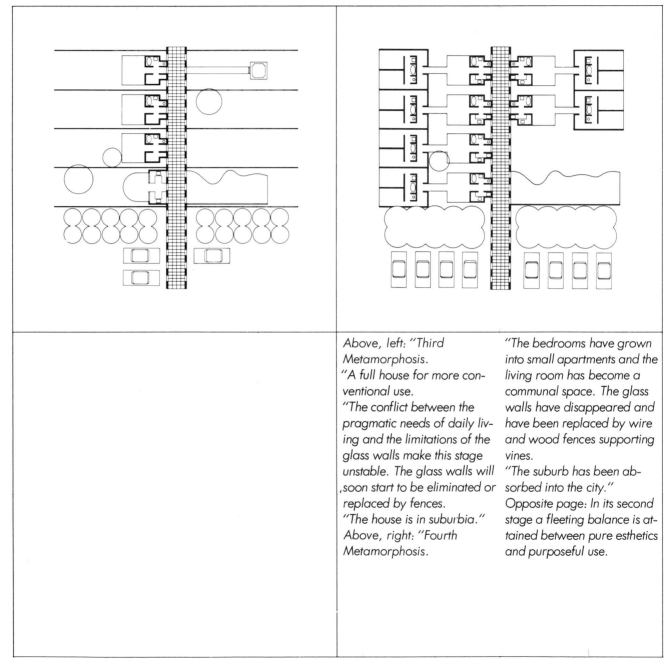

Above, left: "Third Metamorphosis.

"A full house for more conventional use.

"The conflict between the pragmatic needs of daily living and the limitations of the glass walls make this stage unstable. The glass walls will ,soon start to be eliminated or replaced by fences.

"The house is in suburbia."

Above, right: "Fourth Metamorphosis.

"The bedrooms have grown into small apartments and the living room has become a communal space. The glass walls have disappeared and have been replaced by wire and wood fences supporting vines.

"The suburb has been absorbed into the city."

Opposite page: In its second stage a fleeting balance is attained between pure esthetics and purposeful use.

A hypothetical design for an exhibition titled "Suburban and Urban Alternatives," displayed by the Venice Biennale Organization from July 31 to October 10, 1976. The site and program were left for the entrants to devise, and the design response is best described by the architect's statements accompanying the fourfold sequence of plans.

Left: Residential tower from Fifth Avenue. The glass skin will be composed of soft shades of blue and gray. Opposite page: North elevation. The lighter colored right portion of the tower is a leg of the L-shaped plan resulting from a legal agreement with an adjoining property owner. The stepped top is a bow to New York tradition.

Museum of Modern Art

No other project is ever likely to bring Pelli as much recognition or as much criticism as this immensely demanding one. Controversy was assured by the client's decision to double the Museum of Modern Art's exhibit space and finance that expansion through sale of air rights for a revenue-producing apartment tower.

There will be gains and losses. On one hand, the museum will be able to expand its services, operate more efficiently, and show more art in a more conveniently arranged series of galleries. On the other hand, fine old buildings will be removed from 53rd Street and replaced by a huge tower, forever changing the scale and character of that block.

But these credits and debits arise from the program and circumstances rather than from the architect. How well the tower and museum expansion turn out will be a test of Pelli's ability to deal with serious political, economic, legal, social, and structural complications as well as issues of pure design. Indeed, a major factor in his selection was that only he among leading architects was thought capable of making all the necessary concessions and compromises and still have a work of architecture left in the end.

Inevitably, the towering tail will wag the dog. To soften that effect, the apartments have been given a stepped top in deference to an older New York practice, and a legally mandated vertical notch at the rear will lend elegant asymmetry to the north face. The design has been called ambiguous, but perhaps it is only subtle. Pelli is again working at the expressive edge of skins, this time by weaving different colors of glass and mullions into a cool, complex pattern whose success can only be judged at full scale once the tower is built.

The museum portion is still undergoing final design refinements, and if it will be less than dazzling, it will be out of concern for an already variegated whole rather than for lack of imaginative effort. The enlarged museum cannot repeat the simple coup of the 1939 original, but it may contribute to a gentler definition of modernism.

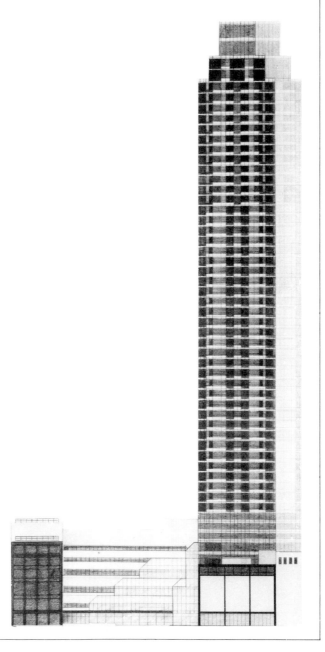

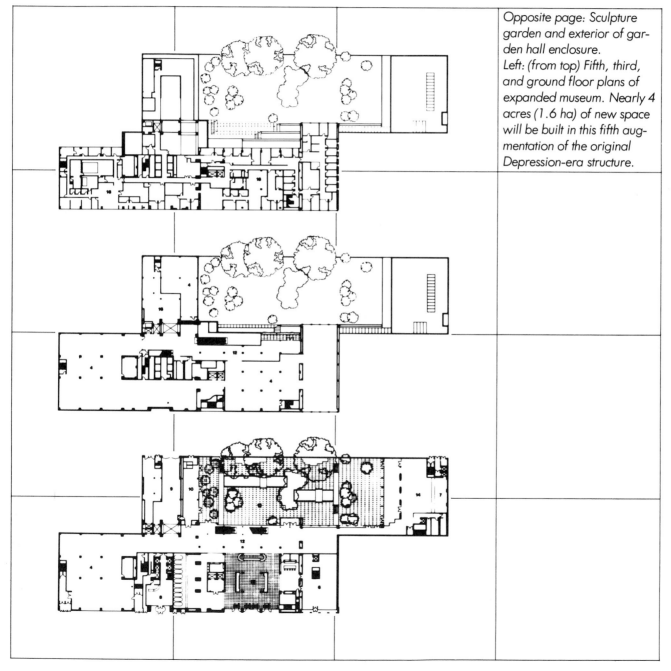

Opposite page: Sculpture garden and exterior of garden hall enclosure.
Left: (from top) Fifth, third, and ground floor plans of expanded museum. Nearly 4 acres (1.6 ha) of new space will be built in this fifth augmentation of the original Depression-era structure.

Opposite page: Garden hall from third floor. This stepped, glass-walled, four-story space will give the upper museum floors generous garden and city views while adding drama to the journey from one level to another.
Above: The museum's residential tower, at 56 stories, is one of Manhattan's tallest midblock buildings.
Following pages:
Page 110: Combining two colors of mullions with several muted shades of glass, the residential tower curtain wall is Pelli's most complex essay in a favorite form.
Page 111: View across 53rd Street. The lower portion of the tower was designed to be less prominent than the original museum facade at right-center, but the 650-ft-tall (200-m) new structure will inevitably dominate all but the most proximate views.

Site: An irregular 1.8 acre (.7 ha) midblock on West 53 and 54 Streets, between 5th and 6th Avenues. Most of the property is occupied by existing museum structures and gardens that will be retained. Buildings: A new, 500,000-sq-ft (46,452-sq-m) condominium tower of 56 stories, with exterior volume, skin, and public lobby designed by Pelli. The museum will have 270,000 sq ft (25,084 sq m) of renovated space and 167,000 sq ft (15,515 sq m) of new area within an 8-story structure of which 6 are above ground. Sale of the museum's unused development rights to a separate Tower Corporation will finance the expansion, while the tower's payment of a yearly sum in lieu of property taxes will subsidize the museum's operating costs. Materials and cost: The tower has a reinforced concrete structural frame and is clad in tinted and opaque glass. The museum's structure is primarily reinforced concrete, and its exterior is glass and marble. Costs are estimated at $60 million for the tower and $20 million for the museum in 1980.

Clients: The Museum of Modern Art and the Trust for Cultural Resources.

Hermann Park Towers

Cesar Pelli earned this commission by winning an invitational competition, and of all his current projects, it seems to be the boldest step beyond previous work. Hermann Park Towers express in unfettered form a romanticism that has usually been implicit in his best buildings. Possibly emboldened by postmodernist examples, he allows his design liberties that would have been unlikely a few years earlier. In their unabashed sensuousness of form, surprisingly knowing use of so old-fashioned a material as brick masonry, and Beaux-Arts symmetry of site plan, the Hermann Towers yield to intuition, setting, and tradition all at once. Their forms are hauntingly familiar, faintly anthropomorphic, and unmistakably resortlike.

Their welcome lyricism is accompanied by games and surprises. One tower is half again as tall as its mate, and the mind's eye wants to connect their corresponding bumps and corners with spidery radiating lines. The opposing walls of this graceful Mutt and Jeff are not flowing but rather cleaved flat with surgical neatness and startling dispassion. Were these two once one?

The dichotomy of stern flatness and buoyant modulation brings satisfying tension to a design that might otherwise have been too soft in form and spirit. It also makes Hermann Park Towers a Janus-like symbol of Cesar Pelli's efforts to date. One face, tough, rational, and controlled, looks back over a full past. The other, compliant, intuitive, and free, contemplates what may prove to be the future.

Below: Site plan of Hermann Park Towers exhibits a symmetry and order that recalls Italian renaissance gardens. Opposite page: Cesar Pelli considers tall buildings to be symbols of standing people and in no other of his designs is that human metaphor as easy to detect as it is here.

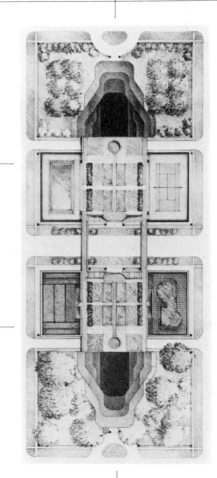

Below: Floor plans of taller tower. Undulating balconies, 200 in number, not only provide outdoor space but also act as sunshades for large windows in an almost tropical climate.
Opposite page: Model of project.

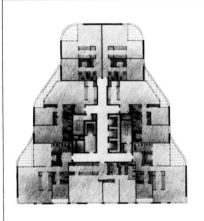

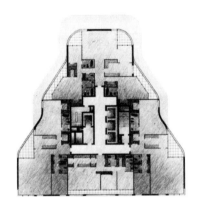

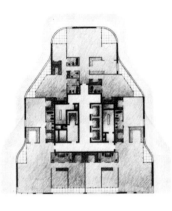

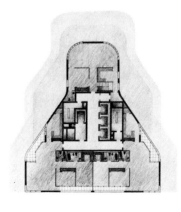

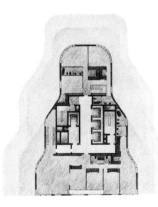

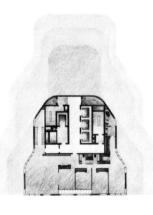

Site: Two city blocks totaling 3.4 acres (1.4 ha) of flat land, facing a large park and bounded by Hermann Drive, Crawford Blvd., Binz Avenue, and Jackson Street, in an older district 2.5 miles (4 km) south of downtown Houston.

Buildings: Two towers of 18 and 30 stories, containing a total of 246 condominium apartments. Gardens and recreational facilities occupy the roof of two garages providing 426 parking spaces.

Materials and cost: Flat slab reinforced concrete structural system, with exterior brick cavity walls and operable windows of tinted glass. Cost is estimated at $35 million in 1980.

Client: Hermann Park, Inc.

Chronology

The following is a selective chronology of Cesar Pelli's work after his decade in Eero Saarinen's office. Projects are listed by year of design, while actual construction dates range from one to seven years later.

DANIEL, MANN, JOHNSON & MENDENHALL

1965

Chevron Office Building Proposal
El Segundo, California
Design team leader: Philo Jacobson
Not built

International Jewelry Center
Beverly Hills, California
In collaboration with: Anthony Lumsden

Roosevelt Building Renovation
Los Angeles, California

Sunset Mountain Park
Santa Monica, California
In collaboration with: Anthony Lumsden
Design team leader: Philo Jacobson
Not built

1966

Century City Medical Plaza
Los Angeles, California
In collaboration with: Anthony Lumsden

Federal Building
Lawndale, California
In collaboration with: Anthony Lumsden
Design team leader: Philo Jacobson

General Telephone Building
Santa Monica, California
Design team leader: Philo Jacobson

Kodak Lab
Hollywood, California

Lockheed
Sunnyvale, California
Not built

Teledyne Labs
Northridge, California
In collaboration with: Anthony Lumsden
Design team leader: Philo Jacobson

Wil-Selby Apartment House Complex
Los Angeles, California
Design team leader: William Mateson
Not built

Worldway Postal Center
Los Angeles, California
In collaboration with: Anthony Lumsden

1967

Ala Wai Plaza
Honolulu, Hawaii
Design team leader: Richard Tipping

COMSAT Laboratory
Clarksburg, Maryland
Design team leader: Philo Jacobson

Kukui Housing
Honolulu, Hawaii
Design team leaders: Lance Bird and Richard Tipping

St. Vincent's Hospital
Los Angeles, California
Designers: Lance Bird and Douglas Meyer

Third Street Tunnel
Los Angeles, California
In collaboration with: Anthony Lumsden
Design team leader: Richard Mattieson

1968

California Jewelry Mart
Los Angeles, California
Design team leader: Bruce Miller

GRUEN ASSOCIATES

1968

Pacific Centre
Vancouver, British Columbia
Toronto Dominion Bank
Eaton's Department Store
Partner in charge: William Dahl
Design team leader: Miloyko Lazovich

1969

Beef'n Counter
Mid-Wilshire District
Los Angeles, California
Design team leader: Arthur Golding

Manchester Lease
Clayton, Missouri
Design team leader: Arthur Golding

San Bernardino City Hall
San Bernardino, California
Design team leader: Lance Bird

Simpson's Court/Simpson's Department Store
Sherway Gardens
(Department Store Balcony Restaurant)
Yorkdale, Toronto, Ontario, Canada
Design team leader: George Spacek

Snowmass at Aspen Proposal
Aspen, Colorado
Design team leader: Douglas Meyer
Not built

UN City
International Competition
International Organizations Headquarters
and Conference Centre in Vienna, Austria
Design team: Cesar Pelli, partner;
Roylance Bird, Jr., Richard Dodson, Arthur Golding,
Friedrich Kastner, Doug Meyer, Victor Schumacher, Engelbert Zobl
Not built

Western Electric/Gateway II
Newark, New Jersey
Partner in charge: Abbott Harle
Design team leader: Geoffrey Freeman

1970

Commons/Courthouse Center
Columbus, Ohio
Design team leader: Lance Bird
Designer: Victor Schumacher
Project manager: Antal Borsa

Laguna Niguel Museum
Laguna Niguel, California
Design team leader: Lance Bird
Not built

Ohrbachs Del Amo
Del Amo, California
Design team leader: Miloyko Lazovich

Santa Anita Fashion Park
Santa Anita, California
Partner in charge: Edgardo Contini
Design team leader: George Spacek

Security Pacific National Bank
San Bernardino, California
Designers: Diana Balmori and Douglas Meyer

White Front Project
Discount Stores
Southern California
Design team leader: Arthur Golding
Not built

1971

Naval Facilities Engineering Command
Long Beach, California
Partner in charge: William Dahl
Designer: Douglas Meyer

Oakland City Center
Oakland, California
Wells Fargo Building

Partner in charge: Karl van Leuven
Design team leader: Lance Bird
Designer: Victor Schumacher

Ohrbachs Cerritos
Cerritos, California
Design team leader: Miloyko Lazovich

Pacific Design Center
Los Angeles, California
Partners in charge: Edgardo Contini and Alan Rubenstein
Design team leader: Miloyko Lazovich

Park Center Financial Plaza
San Jose, California
United California Bank
Partner in charge: Herman Gutman
Design team leader: Charles Jones

1972

Ten Eyck Blocks
Albany, New York
Partner in charge: Abbott Harle

U.S. Embassy
Tokyo, Japan
Design team leader: Arthur Golding
Designer: Fred Clarke
Project Manager: Rolf Sklarek

1973

Fox Hills Mall
Culver City, California
Partner in charge: Edgardo Contini
Design team leader: Arthur Golding

Oakland City Center
Oakland, California
Clorox Building
Partner in charge: Karl van Leuven
Design team leader: Lance Bird
Designer: Victor Schumacher

City of Industry City Hall
City of Industry, California

Design team leader: Fred Clarke
Not built

Zurich American Insurance Co.
Moorestown, New Jersey
Partner in charge: Beda Zwicker
Design team leader: Geoffrey Freeman

1974

Lauritsen Laboratory
China Lake, California
Design team leader: Heinz Meyer

Yale School of Music
New Haven, Connecticut
Associate in charge: Fred Clarke
Design team leader: Arthur Golding
Not built

1975

Rainbow Center Mall/Winter Garden
Niagara Falls, New York
Partner in charge: Abbott Harle
Design team leader: Gary Engel

1976

Daehan Kyoyuk Insurance Co.
Seoul, Korea
Partner in charge: Edgardo Contini
Design team leader: Fred Clarke

Biennale House
"Suburban and Urban Alternatives Exhibition"
Venice, Italy—Biennale Organization
31 July to 10 October
Design team leader: Fred Clarke
Not built

CESAR PELLI & ASSOCIATES

1977

Museum of Modern Art—Renovation & Tower

New York
CP&A in association with:
Gruen Associates, P.C.
   New York
Llewelyn-Davies Associates
   New York
Edward Durrell Stone Associates, P.C.
   New York
Designers: Fred Clarke, Diana Balmori, Thomas Morton

1978

U.S. Embassy Renovation
Havana, Cuba
Design team leader: Diana Balmori
Not built

1979

Bunker Hill Redevelopment Plan and
Office Building Competition
Los Angeles, California
Associate in charge: Fred Clarke
Designer: Jon Pickard

Four Leaf Towers
Houston, Texas
Associate in charge: Fred Clarke
Design team leader: Randall Mudge

Four Stamford Forum
Stamford, Connecticut
Associate in charge: Fred Clarke
Design team leader: Douglas Denes
Project manager: Bruce Sielaff
Job captain: Howard Howes

Gewirz House
Glen Echo, Maryland
Associate in charge: Fred Clarke
Designers: Jon Pickard and Robert Charney

Hermann Park Towers
Houston, Texas
Associate in charge: Fred Clarke
Design team leader: Randall Mudge
Designer: Gregg Jones

Oliver Tyrone III—Proposal
Pittsburgh, Pennsylvania
Associate in charge: Fred Clarke
Not built

Pin Oak (Master Plan)
Houston, Texas
Associate in charge: Fred Clarke

900 Third Avenue
New York
Associate in charge: Fred Clarke
Design team leader: Tom Morton
Designer: Kevin Hart

1980

California State Office Building at
Sacramento, California
Associate in charge: Fred Clarke

Chicago Tribune Competition
Chicago, Illinois
Associate in charge: Fred Clarke
Designer: Turan Duda
Not built

Cleveland Clinic
Cleveland, Ohio
Associate in charge: Fred Clarke
Project architect: Bruce Sielaff
Design team leader: Mac Ball
Designer: James Baird

Crown Center Office Building
Kansas City, Missouri
Associate in charge: Fred Clarke
Design team leader: Jon Pickard
Designer: Karen Cornelius

One State Street Proposal
Hartford, Connecticut
Associate in charge: Fred Clarke
Not built

CREDITS

Unless noted by an asterisk * below, all artwork has been supplied courtesy
Cesar Pelli & Associates. The list includes the work of both
photographers and renderers, with renderers noted.

Mac Ball (renderer), 96 (left)
William E. Butler (renderer), 96 (right), 114
Ken Champlin, 104, 110, 115
Fred Clarke, 36 (below), 75
*Herbert Bruce Cross, 25
Turan Duda (renderer), 99
*Dean Dablow, courtesy Jean Ferriss Leich, 92
Arthur Golding, 40, 58
*Gruen Associates, 19, 32, 64, 65 (top), 71,
72, 73 (right), 76, 78, 90 (left)
Stephen Hill, 46 (top), 47
Howard Assoc. (renderer), 108
Wolfgang Hoyt-Esto, 108
*© The Japan Architect, Masao Arai (photographer),
88 (left), 89 (below)
*© The Japan Architect, Mitsuo Matsuoka (photographer),
88 (top)
*Balthazar Korab, 31 (left),34, 50, 53, 61, 63 (top), 67, 75
*Nathaniel Lieberman, 33
*Norman McGrath, 77-79
*Mitsuo Matsuoka, 86, 89 (above)
Tom Morton (renderer), 105
*John Pastier, 36-37, 52, 55, 68, 85
Jon Pickard (renderer), 14, 22, 93, 94-95, 97,
99 (left), 113
*Marvin Rand, 39, 40-41, 81, 82, 83 (top), 84 (left
and above)
Naomi Rutenberg, 2
*Julius Shulman, 28-29
J. Severtson, K. Champlin, 106, 109, 111
Barry Zauss (renderer), 54

The following names were inadvertently omitted
from the Chronology:

Four-Leaf Towers
Associated Architects: A. C. Martin & Associates

900 Third Avenue
Associated Architects: Rafael Viñoly, Gruen Associates, P.C.

California State Office Building
Associated Architects: Fisher-Friedman

Cleveland Clinic
Associated Architects: Dalton, van Dijk, Johnson